'I'm someone who prides themself on being on top of their organisation game, so to speak, so I was curious to see what clever tips and tricks I could learn – I literally could not put Lorraine's book down. I began to make changes and implemented so many of her suggestions – they were easy to put into practice, with a huge, immediate payoff.

It's the best feeling to know you're in charge of how your day plays out, and not being at the mercy of external forces. The way Lorraine writes is so personable and relatable, you feel immediately like you've got a friend at your side guiding you through.'

Sally Obermeder, television presenter, radio host, bestselling author, Co-founder and Creative Director at SWIISH

'Lorraine is in a class of her own as a thought leader, and her wise, down-to-earth words have helped this previously disorganised journalist actually manage to get her act together. Lorraine's first title, *Remarkability*, is one of those books that I always keep in the "front section" of my ginormous book shelf, so that says it all!'

Libby-Jane Charleston, Associate Editor at HuffPost

'Lorraine has been working with my business via her mentoring program for the past twelve months. In this time we have focused on getting (and keeping) me super organised to run a cracking business. We've made sure that as the company grows, I've got all the right frameworks in place for success. We've also made sure I'm organised enough to fit in my monthly hair appointment – locking them in twelve months in advance! Sheer brilliance.'

Jacqui Daley, Founder and Managing Director at The Measured Marketer

T0304947

'Lorraine has given me a practical, systematic and realistic approach to get both my business and my life so seriously organised that I was able to clear the decks and have time and headspace to actually get shit done. Lorraine tackles goal setting and productivity, as well as helpful life hacks that have made a huge difference to the speed of growth of our small business.'

Mike Blackwell, Owner and Principal at Fix Physio

'I thought I was pretty organised. I have military training and can make up a faultless bed in ninety seconds. So when I met Lorraine it was great to find someone who could manage an awesome career whilst still having some free time. Victory, I thought! What I didn't realise is that living with Lorraine is like having a mirror up to your productivity. Nowadays, Alexis and I have come to grips with our goal-setting, routines and life productivity – and couldn't be happier.'

Wade Tink, Lorraine's husband, General Manager
and Director at Project Everest

Get REMARKABLY Organised

LORRAINE MURPHY

hachette
AUSTRALIA

hachette
AUSTRALIA

Published in Australia and New Zealand in 2018
by Hachette Australia
(an imprint of Hachette Australia Pty Limited)
Level 17, 207 Kent Street, Sydney NSW 2000
www.hachette.com.au

10 9 8 7 6 5 4 3

Copyright © Lorraine Murphy 2018

NATIONAL
LIBRARY
OF AUSTRALIA

A catalogue record for this
book is available from the
National Library of Australia

ISBN: 978 0 7336 3948 7 (paperback)

Cover design by Grace West
Cover images courtesy of Shutterstock
Text design by Kirby Jones
Typeset in Sabon LT and Helvetica Neue by Kirby Jones
Printed and bound in Great Britain by Clays Ltd, Elcograf S.p.A.

MIX
Paper from
responsible sources
FSC® C104740
www.fsc.org

To Lexi's morning naps – without you this book
would not have been possible.

Contents

About this book

When I wrote my first book, *Remarkability*, I had certain assumptions about which chapters would resonate most with people – particularly the early-stage entrepreneurs that I had in mind as I was writing.

The chapter on sales I thought would be a sure winner – doesn't everyone want to make more money for their business? Also up there on my mental list was the chapter on leadership, and definitely the one on goal-setting.

The book went on to be a bestseller – sitting in the top ten business books chart for twelve weeks straight. I received hundreds of cards, social media comments and emails from readers of the book expressing their gratitude for the experiences I had shared in it. I also got to meet many readers face to face at various speaking events.

I was blown away when I asked the question: 'Which chapter was your favourite?'

Time and time again, people replied: 'The chapter on getting organised.' This was generally quickly followed by some combination of 'I really struggle with that', 'I'm hopelessly disorganised' or 'I desperately need some help on that front'.

Happily, many of these readers were already actioning some of the simple tips I'd shared in 'Get Seriously F*cking Organised' – and were already feeling the benefits of tiny, repetitive actions done every day. They were feeling more in control of their lives, more motivated and definitely calmer.

It got me thinking about the lives we lead today that result in us feeling like we're constantly chasing our tails. And this is not solely the burden of entrepreneurs!

Between the demands of careers/businesses, partners, families, friends, staying healthy and squeezing in some time to have fun, it seems that many of us are really struggling to keep up with it all ... whether we have our own business or not.

Add in the always-on factor of now having smartphones within one metre of us for most (if not all) of our days and I realised that we have very little opportunity to think and plan ahead. We have an endless stream of information at our fingertips with these self-same phones – have you noticed how no one sits and waits while doing nothing anymore?

I went to the bathroom after seeing a movie recently, and I couldn't believe it when I came out of the Ladies to find that *every single person* in the cinema lobby was absorbed in their phones (including my husband!).

While we're at it, let's pile on the demands of social media. I don't know about you, but I find it incredibly difficult to stay present with the advent of Instagram Stories. When I find I have a spare couple of minutes, I default to looking around for something to post about – content that will be non-existent in just twenty-four hours.

Suffice to say, our lives are more action-packed, plugged in and fast-paced than any other period in the history of humankind.

The result is that many of us feel we are constantly in reactive mode – that we're spending all of our days responding to external forces; from the aforementioned business/family/ etc. to traffic, from a stack of bills to be paid to phone calls, from making a meeting on time to a bursting email inbox.

Personally, I know I constantly have a mental list running – which after a while gets really bloody exhausting. I firmly believe that there's a better way to live – a way that puts us back in control of our lives, and means we feel we're making progress – rather than simply treading water every day in an effort to stay afloat.

It seems that the 4000 words I wrote on addressing this problem by getting seriously organised in *Remarkability* had a profound effect on many people. What I thought were pretty simple tips had a transformational effect on their lives.

Readers have told me that they're feeling as if they are in the driving seat again, and motivated to get out there and smash their goals. They send me little updates on their organisational wins – like 'I made my lunch the night before for the first time EVER', to 'I've seriously never been so productive in my life'.

It's been awesome!

And it's also got me thinking.

If this is the impact just 4000 words had, how much could an entire book help people ... Please welcome *Get Remarkably Organised* with your host, yours truly.

This book is based on similar principles to that lone chapter in *Remarkability*; however, I have delved into much more detail within these pages.

Like anyone, my approach is constantly evolving and in this book I'll also share my new discoveries since writing *Remarkability* that are helping me feel more 'on top' of life. At the end of each chapter, you'll find a GRO (Get Remarkably Organised) list. These are my suggestions to help you absorb the key take-outs from that chapter, and get you started at actioning them in your own life – today.

But wait, there's more!

I am not so egotistical (I hope …) to think that it's my way or the highway. After all, one person's trash is another person's treasure! So, rather than base this whole book on my advice, I decided to interview some remarkable people and ask them how *they* organise their lives. The responses in these interviews have been utterly fascinating – and I've already adopted some of their tips in my own life.

You'll also hear how readers of *Remarkability* have adapted my suggestions into *their* own lives – with remarkable success.

Before we get started, however, I'd like you to take a few minutes to do some thinking.

In the military, there is a concept called 'Commander's Intent' and it is at the core of a successful exercise. There are three steps to Commander's Intent:

1. Purpose – *why* the exercise is being undertaken.
2. Method – *how* the exercise will be undertaken.
3. Endstate – the *result* desired at the end of the exercise.

Take a minute or two to think about your *purpose* for picking up this book. Why do you want to become remarkably organised? Write it down here or in a notebook.

_____

_____

_____

_____

_____

_____

The *method* is the book you have in your hands. Now ask yourself about your *endstate*. What do you want your life to look like once you've successfully applied the method to your life? How do you feel about your life?

_____

_____

_____

_____

_____

_____

I hope that in this book you unlock a whole new level of structure that will put you in the driving seat to make the life of your dreams a reality.

Now, let's get seriously fucking organised ...

PART ONE

LET'S GET SERIOUSLY FUCKING ORGANISED

CHAPTER 1

What is 'being organised'?

Let's get started on this journey to organisational bliss with a bit of a chat about what it actually *means* to be organised.

Take a moment to conjure up a vision of the type of human you think of when I say 'an organised person'. I would venture to guess that it may not be the most positive of images – am I right?

I know I used to believe that an organised person was someone whose Filofax was permanently tucked under their arm, and whose their life was governed by said Filofax. Flash forward a few years, and you could sub in Google Calendar for the leather-bound organiser.

Or maybe it's someone whose entire day is scheduled down to the last minute, and they move robotically from one appointment to the next, with little joy involved in the whole exercise.

When we think of organised people, we don't necessarily think of dynamic, fun individuals. It's as if we have deeply ingrained archetypes of what it means to be organised, and if we ourselves don't match one of those archetypes, then all hope is lost and we'll never be able to wrangle a sense of order into our lives. I would even venture to say that until very recently, being organised was not cool!

There has been something of a zeitgeist when it comes to organisation in recent years, which again underlines how challenging daily life has become for the vast majority of us. For the reasons I mentioned in the previous chapter, we desperately want to feel more in control of our lives.

Books like *The Life-Changing Magic of Tidying Up* and *Getting Things Done* have become global bestsellers, and there has been a dramatic increase in the popularity of get-your-life-sorted products such as those you find on the shelves of kikki.K. It's becoming rather trendy to be organised, and – as a self-confessed organisational nerd – I couldn't be happier about that!

Being organised does not equate to being obsessed. And nor should it.

If you are feeling organised, you will probably feel like:

- You have a strong working knowledge of what's coming up today, this week and this month.
- You're approaching your days and tasks with a sense of purpose.
- Your 'monkey mind' is kept in check as you have a handle on your to-do list.
- You can enjoy periods of downtime as you know you have factored in when you're going to achieve your key priorities.

- You're generally using your time and energy towards productive means.
- You're in control and periods of being overwhelmed are not the norm for you.
- Generally speaking, your default setting is one of calm.

This isn't you right now?

Please don't worry. That's why we're spending this time together and no doubt the reason you picked up this book.

In the following chapters, we're going to delve into various areas of organisation – from routines and to-do lists to priority management. If you've read my first book, *Remarkability*, you'll know that I pride myself on being organised – and in fact I credit that approach with much of my success and enjoyment with my business and other areas of my life.

I have spent a *lot* of time studying, practising and thinking about how to be more organised – and in all of that, I have realised that there is one uniting principle that underpins the concept of being an organised person. It's a common thread that I've seen not just in the individual tactics of being organised, but also in real-life examples of the successful people I interviewed for this book.

All the daily planners, diarising, routines and to-do lists in the world won't help us if we don't grasp this one principle. Until we 'get' it, our approach to organisation will at best be disjointed and at worst result in failure – which again reinforces our belief that we can never be one of those 'organised types'.

In fact, I believe that if you can grasp this one principle and practise it every single day of your life, you will dramatically reduce the need for any of the other tips and tricks we'll go through together in the pages to come.

So, let me introduce …

The principle of your Future Self

It's become a popular joke to say, 'That will be Future Me's problem' when we have created an especially tricky problem that we will ultimately need to deal with.

For example, I order that extra bottle of wine knowing that I have an important meeting the next morning. That's Future Lorraine's problem. Then when the next morning rolls around and I'm hating my life hard, I really wish that Past Lorraine had given me some consideration approximately ten hours beforehand.

Or I might procrastinate on starting work on the PowerPoint presentation for a new business offer, knowing that I made a commitment to send it to the client the following week. I'll potter about in my email inbox, check social media and tidy my desk – and generally work on trivial, non-time-sensitive tasks – all the while telling myself that Future Lorraine can deal with the presentation next week. And, yep, you guessed it – next week Future Lorraine is not the world's biggest fan of Past Lorraine!

If we flip this joke on its head and use it to our advantage, the results can be staggering.

> Rather than deferring tasks to our Future Selves, if we can instead *take care of* our Future Selves by making their lives that little bit easier, life overall starts to flow more smoothly.

I had an 'aha' moment a few months ago that all the 'stuff' I do to stay organised – the meal planning, the structured to-do lists, the task batching, the habit layering – all if it, without exception, is geared at helping my Future Self.

Conversely, in the times I'm feeling stressed, overwhelmed, behind schedule or under pressure, it's because in some way I didn't watch out for my Future Self.

I'll give you two quite different examples from just the last two months as I wrote this chapter.

Myself and the team had commissioned a major piece of research, and were about to share it with key clients and media at two breakfast events – first in Sydney and then in Melbourne.

On the morning of the Sydney event, I had my hair and make-up done at the dining table while I did some last-minute swotting on my notes. I was very nervous about this first event as we had 120 paying guests and my keynote presentation was mostly made up of complex charts and statistics, which is not my usual speaking style. It was also my first time presenting the data.

We had a lot of content to get through, so we made it very clear in communication in the run-up to the day itself that the presentation would be starting at 7.30 a.m. – and so guests needed to be smack-bang on time.

Even though the hair and make-up artist was on my doorstep at 6 a.m., I hadn't factored in enough time for her to work her magic, eat some breakfast, get changed and walk the ten minutes to the venue. I had planned to arrive at the hotel just before 7 a.m., but I was now running twenty minutes behind schedule. I knew there was a venue filling up with people – and I wasn't there to help the team with the final stages of setting up.

At 7.10 a.m. I raced downstairs and as I did so I smashed my brand new (and expensive) make-up compact. I was so wound up as I left the house that I forgot my phone – so I had to turn back when I was halfway to the hotel to get it. I arrived at 7.25 a.m. and found that the hotel staff hadn't got the room set up yet, so had to switch into full-on 'we need shit done RIGHT NOW!' mode.

We finally started at 7.45 a.m., and I felt frazzled and distracted as I took to the stage – not to mention feeling rather embarrassed that after the guests had turned up on time, it was the event organisers who were running late.

Thankfully, I settled down once we got underway; however, I was angry with myself for not being kinder to Future Lorraine by allowing more time and getting up half an hour earlier. This in turn would have meant I was kinder to my team and the venue staff, and everyone's morning would have been dramatically more pleasant.

A non-business related – and totally superficial – example happened just last week. I was due to fly to Melbourne for three intense days of meetings and my hair needed a solid wash. As my meetings on the first day were quite informal, I decided not to bother going to the effort of washing my hair on the morning I flew out of Sydney and instead scraped it up into a bun.

Washing my hair would be Future Lorraine's problem and I'd do it the following morning while I was in Melbourne. This meant I had to pack the various products and accoutrements required for the hair-washing exercise, which made my suitcase heavier.

The next morning rolled around and (of course) Melbourne offered one of its signature chilly mornings. I hauled myself out of bed and braved the cold bathroom, then found that the apartment I was staying in had probably the worst water pressure I'd experienced in recent memory. It took three times as long to wash my hair, and I was cursing myself for not just doing it the day before in the comfort of my balmy Sydney bathroom and powerful shower.

When it came to drying my hair, I found that the hairdryer provided in the apartment didn't do heat – so I dried my hair with cold air. This again took triple the amount of time it usually does and blasting my wet hair with chilly air on a cold day wasn't exactly a pleasant experience!

The result of me deferring a pretty unremarkable task to Future Lorraine was that I lost thirty minutes on that morning. This meant I had to grab a quick breakfast in the lobby of the corporate company with which I was meeting, while making some last tweaks to my presentation as I ate, rather than enjoying my usual go-to breakfast spot in Melbourne and adding some more creative flourishes to my slides. The hair-washing experience at home would have been infinitely more pleasant than the one I had in Melbourne, and I also had to lug a couple of kilos of hair products around with me in my suitcase.

These two situations proved to me yet again that when I act in the present moment and just do something then and there – no matter how small it might be – it saves my Future Self hassle. And in just that simple action, I immediately feel more on top of things.

I have built this concept into every area of my life:

- I pull out all the clothes I need for the following day before I go to bed every night – including exercise gear if that's on the day's agenda.
- I have that difficult business conversation today, so that Future Lorraine doesn't arrive in the office tomorrow or next week with her shoulders sagging knowing that she needs to do it.
- I wash up the items I've used to prepare dinner as I use them, so that after dinner Future Lorraine can just kick back and relax.
- I make a start on a presentation that's due days before I need to – even if it's just creating the PowerPoint document, titling the slides and saving it.
- I book regular appointments a year in advance so that Future Lorraine doesn't have to go to the dentist at a stupidly disruptive time like 2 p.m. on a Tuesday because that's the only time the dentist now has available.

All of these things ladder up to a general sense of calm – and the more I embed the principle of the Future Self into my life, the calmer life gets. And it's not just me who has embraced it. Some of the most successful people I know do the very same thing – even if they don't quite realise that what they're actually doing is looking after their Future Selves.

My dear friend Lisa Messenger pre-arranges for one of her team to put a green smoothie on her desk when she arrives in the office in the morning. She describes it as 'her only Anna Wintour thing'. Knowing that she'll have that hit of goodness sets her up for the day, and means that Future Lisa doesn't need to be as concerned about the food on offer at the various functions she attends most days.

Tony Robbins states that one of his biggest learnings has been to never leave the scene of setting a goal without doing one thing to get him closer to that goal. It might be putting a meeting in his diary or calling a potential mentor to make first contact with them – anything to start some flow. He knows that by taking the very first – and the most difficult – step towards that goal, Future Tony will find it easier to keep the momentum going and see that goal through to reality.

As we embark on this adventure towards organisation together, we'll work through a wide range of tools that you can apply to your life straight away to help you get back in the driving seat. You'll see that the Future Self Principle will be woven throughout many of these tools.

Give your Future Self some TLC right now, today, and enjoy the benefits it brings.

The GRO list

1. Identify two examples in the last month of how you looked after your Future Self and noticed a positive impact by doing so.
2. Spot two examples in the last month of how life became unnecessarily fraught due to not looking out for your Future Self.
3. List three things you could do every day to help your Future Self the following day.

CHAPTER 2

Declutter

The first step in getting remarkably organised is to get rid of 'stuff'. I firmly believe that the amount of physical clutter we have directly correlates with how much mental clutter we have.

Ever notice how when you've got a major work deadline looming that for some reason you tidy your desk, organise the files on your computer and deal with all your fiddly annoying admin? Or when you were at school or uni, that you spent *hours* tidying your room rather than studying for an exam – much to your parents' frustration?

Our brains need clear physical space in order to think clearly, and all the crap that every one of us accumulates gradually builds up to erode this ability.

Excess things in your surroundings can have a negative impact on your ability to focus and process information.

When neuroscientists at Princeton University looked at people's task performance in an organised versus disorganised environment, they found that physical clutter in participants' surroundings competed for their attention, resulting in decreased performance and increased stress. The annoyance of clutter also wore down their mental resources and they were more likely to become frustrated.[1]

In another study, a team of UCLA researchers recently observed thirty-two families in Los Angeles and found that all of the mothers' stress hormones spiked during the time they spent dealing with their belongings. Similar to what multitasking does to your brain, physical clutter overloads your senses, making you feel stressed, and impairs your ability to think creatively.[2]

The conclusions were strong – if you want to focus to the best of your ability and process information as effectively as possible, you need to clear the clutter from your home and work environment. The research shows that you will be less irritable, more productive, distracted less often, and able to process information better with an uncluttered and organised home and office.

Case in point: the night before I was due to sit down and kick start this book properly.

We had moved house three months earlier. Two weeks after the house move, the team and I moved out of the office we had been in for eighteen months.

We had a two-week period of working remotely before moving into our new business space, so my new home office was the temporary holding pen of the various office supplies we decided we *absolutely needed* after a savage cull of the many storage areas in the old office.

Life was full with all the moving around and my home office was the last area to be fully unpacked and tidied. Three large plastic tubs worth of 'office stuff' was stacked in the cupboards, along with various stationery and books scattered on the bookshelves.

Weekend after weekend, I told myself this was the time I'd finally tackle the mess – however, it was all so unappealing. As you've probably experienced yourself, decluttering gets a *lot* worse before it gets better and I just couldn't psyche myself up for the task.

To make the situation more unsavoury, I couldn't find my passport after the house move. I was *fairly* sure it was in my home office somewhere, but without physically seeing it I couldn't be 100 per cent sure. I had a trip back to Ireland for my sister's wedding in less than three months, so it was taking up mental headspace rehearsing sorting out a replacement passport if my original one was indeed AWOL.

How would I get a replacement passport? How long would it take? I'd need to get new photos, find the form, make time to fill in the application. And what if the new passport didn't get to me in time? My family would kill me if I missed the wedding.

It came to the evening before my first day starting to write this book, and somehow the motivation to finally deal with my office clutter kicked in. My brain on some level obviously knew it needed to clear the crap before it could focus fully on creating the words you're now reading.

I pulled everything out shelf by shelf and got to work. Three hours, a wheelie bin full of recycling, half a wheelie bin of rubbish and a found passport (hooray!) later, and the office felt like a completely transformed space.

I walked in to write the next morning with clear space around me, and a super-clear mind.

Oprah Winfrey's organisation guru Peter Walsh explains this feeling: 'As ridiculous as it sounds, people feel if they can control their homes and even their closet, this gives them a sense of calm and control ... It's much more about finding peace, calm and motivation in how you live.'[3]

I have experienced the power of decluttering many times.

Over the Christmas–New Year break this year, my husband, Wade, and I went away for nine nights to Vanuatu. We took full advantage of the perspective you get when you're out of the day-to-day routines of business/home/family to talk a lot about where we wanted to be in five years' time, and what we wanted to achieve over the following twelve months.

With our first baby on their way and the plans we each had for our businesses, we realised that we would need a bigger home. Something Wade also wanted to do was cut down on the stuff we had, as he felt that we had accumulated a lot since we moved house two years earlier.

We talked at length about how the true happiness in our lives came from the people and experiences in them, rather than the physical possessions we owned, and we agreed to declutter the house when we got back to Sydney.

I should note here that if you visited our house around this time, you wouldn't have thought it was messy or cluttered. Generally, surfaces were pretty clear and there wasn't crap piled up in the corners. You'd probably think these people were pretty tidy folks and certainly not hoarders.

The true terrors lurked beneath the surface. For example, we had a large three-door storage cupboard that was a huge coup when we moved into this bigger house after being in a 1.5 bedroom cottage for the previous three years. 'So much storage!' we cried – before promptly filling it up with stuff we physically wouldn't have been able to accumulate in our smaller previous house.

In this cupboard were six empty 1-litre beer bottles that Wade had been saving for a friend who home brews, which of course we had forgotten to take with us every time we visited his house … for the last eighteen months. By the time the declutter rolled around, this friend had stopped using bottles and was now using kegs – so we had stored them for *540 days* for no reason.

Also in this cupboard was a random hat that had been left behind after a party six months earlier (the owner obviously wasn't that attached to it), six large canisters of car-cleaning wipes that Wade had snapped up as a 'bargain' – even though he never has time to clean the car himself – and a couple of bags of paperwork that had been tossed in as we got the house ready to rent over the Christmas break. In these bags were important letters and invoices that eventually attracted late fees due to me not dealing with them in time.

I had heard of Marie Kondo's book *The Life-Changing Magic of Tidying Up* a couple of years before – the book had gone on to become a cult title, with four million copies sold in thirty countries worldwide. From what I understood, it was a game-changer when it came to tackling clutter so – with our mission in mind – I downloaded it to my Kindle and got reading.

The book is essentially Marie's recipe for clearing a space of clutter – and keeping it that way. I took notes as I read and geared up for this 'Epic Declutter' as we labelled it.

The first thing Marie says to do is to book out a full day to tackle your entire house. The reason for this is that too often people declutter in small bursts, so they never feel like they have fully decluttered as there's always another area to do. It's almost like doing a full renovation room by room over a series of years – once you've finished the last room, it's time for the first room to be renovated again!

Marie also says that when you tidy using a piecemeal approach, you never get the 'high' that comes with having your entire home cleared of crap. I must admit, I didn't understand this concept until post–Epic Declutter.

Heeding her advice, we booked out a Sunday in January with the goal of getting the whole house done in one mammoth day.

Another piece of advice Marie gives is to tidy by item category rather than by room, which is very smart.

Take clothes as an example. Our house was a three-storey terrace, so most of our clothes resided in our bedroom on the top floor. Heavy winter coats lived in the previously mentioned storage cupboard. Then on the bottom floor we had a cupboard for trainers, boots and some other clothes that didn't fit elsewhere.

If we tried to tidy room by room, then we wouldn't have full visibility on everything we owned by category – making it impossible to spot double-ups of items and get a picture of how many clothes we truly owned.

Ditto for books – there were books strewn throughout the house; same for papers, cosmetics and random household items ...

We started the decluttering adventure by bringing all of our clothes from around the house into our bedroom, and pulling everything out of our wardrobes and tallboy.

The place was an absolute shitfight.

Up until now, I had prided myself on how few clothes I actually owned. I do a clear-out at the end of summer and winter every year, casting away items I know I won't wear next season, or that are too worn-out to go again. It was only when everything was stacked along the bed and the floor that I realised truly how much stuff I had!

There were a couple of garments that I had fallen in love with when I tried them on but never worn as they just didn't ever match my existing wardrobe. There were some things I loved the look of, but that were uncomfortable to wear, so they never quite made it into an outfit. Or items that had been expensive, so I'd kept them because I felt I *should* wear them at some stage.

Probably the most genius tip that Marie offers is to pick up every single thing and ask yourself: 'Does it spark joy?' If the answer is 'yes', you keep it. If the answer is 'no', it goes. I appreciate that this sounds completely whacky/woo woo/illogical; however, bear with me ...

When you ask yourself this question, you over-ride your rational mind – which will inevitably kick in and tell you all the reasons you *should* keep said item: it was a gift, it will fit one day, now you've been reminded of its existence you'll use it *all the time* ... and so on.

Asking yourself whether it sparks joy doesn't give this niggly voice any airtime – meaning you can be a hell of a lot more ruthless. Successfully employing this tactic throughout your entire home also means that ultimately you will be surrounded by possessions that make you truly happy. Doesn't that sound like a nice place to live?

Watching Wade employ this tactic was one of the funniest things I have seen all year. He brought all his army gear up to the bedroom and began to work through it. He would pick up a camouflage jacket, hold it close to his face and say aloud: 'Does it spark joy?' What followed was either a very impassioned nod (yes), or a slightly sad headshake (no).

The hilarious thing was that – to me – every jacket looked *the very fucking same*! Yet some ended up in the rubbish heap and some were lovingly placed back on hangers. It really struck me that the approach is deeply personal to everyone, and that's precisely why it works.

On and on we went – clothes, books, DVDs, papers, stationery, magazines, Christmas decorations, sports equipment. By 7 p.m. we were done – and completely exhausted. We had six large black garbage bags of rubbish and a car boot full (right to the roof) for the charity shop.

The house was completely transformed.

There was a lighter energy and it felt like air was moving more freely through the rooms. Mentally, we felt an expansiveness that we hadn't experienced before and – as nuts as it sounds – it felt like anything was possible from this clearer, energised space. The sense of order, clarity and freshness was truly remarkable.

Something that I realised when reading *The Life-Changing Magic of Tidying Up* and going through this process is that decluttering has a much larger impact than simply making your home feel tidier.

In the book, Marie explains that tidying their homes can be life-changing for her clients. 'The experience of tidying causes them to become more passionately involved in their work. Some set up their own companies, others change jobs and still others take more interest in their current profession.'4

That same weekend, Wade and I went for a stroll around our neighbourhood and happened across a house for lease. The house was one of a group of five terraces that Wade had been obsessed with since arriving in Sydney – he had often remarked to me as we walked past that those terraces were his dream home.

We enquired on Monday morning, and after a few weeks of negotiations the house was ours. I'm writing now from my gorgeous home office, which I manifested the crap out of by visualising a space exactly like this every day last year – never thinking I would be able to have it so soon.

I am absolutely certain that this house would not have been possible had we not cleared all the baggage out of our lives to make way for it. Marie talks about this a lot in her book – clients of hers who, after decluttering their homes, land their dream job, lose the weight they had been trying to lose for years or meet their perfect partner.

> Excess possessions weigh us down – when we release them from our lives, we create abundant space for new things, experiences or people to enter.

Transformational, hey?

This has incredible significance for every other area of our lives, too.

When decluttering, you might come across a shirt that's in perfectly good condition, but that you haven't worn for two years as it doesn't make you feel happy. You accept that you and that shirt have had your time together, and it's time to part ways – with the shirt heading to the charity shop for someone else to find it … someone who will light up every time they put that same shirt on.

I had an intense 'aha' moment when I considered this on a more elevated scale in my life. If clothes and books aren't necessarily meant to stay with us until the very end of either or both of our lives, then why do we cling with such voracity to other perhaps less tangible elements in our lives, struggling to keep them with us no matter what?

Imagine if we detached from not just the unnecessary possessions we own, but the activities, people, commitments and various other elements that make up our lives? If we gradually eliminated all those things that *don't* spark joy for us?

There is a quote attributed to Renaissance sculptor Michelangelo. When speaking of his famous sculpture *David*, on which he worked for two years at the young age of twenty-six, he said: 'It's easy, you just chip away at everything that isn't David.'

He may or may not have said this; however, the idea of gradually chipping away at all the things we *don't* want or need in our lives, to ultimately only leave what we *do* want and deem important, is a charming and very simple concept for me.

I have nurtured some friendships over the years that – when I was *really* honest with myself – I wasn't enjoying as much as

I used to in the past ... and the other person probably wasn't either!

I would lag on getting back to the person on arranging our next catch-up, feel a sense of obligation on my way to meet them and often come away from the time together feeling drained and cranky. I felt that, in some way, I owed them/me the loyalty of staying friends.

What's the point?

If every garment isn't meant to be with us forever and ever, then maybe friends and acquaintances don't need to be either. Ditto for hobbies, jobs, businesses – anything that takes up time and space in our lives.

I don't know about you, but I find this concept to be incredibly freeing. There's a weightlessness about it – in which we can start to take away the stuff that doesn't work for us anymore, in order to find the stuff that *does* work underneath.

I saw celebrity personal trainer and TV personality Michelle Bridges speak recently, and something she talked about was the need to 'subtract' commitments from her life now that she has a young son.

For me, decluttering my physical possessions gave me permission to allow some friendships that had overstayed their welcome in my life to come to an end. There was no song and dance: I simply didn't valiantly keep up the messaging and catch-up invitations.

I took the same approach – almost unconsciously – to my business. I now ask myself what truly makes me happy in my business, and do my best to work towards that on a daily basis.

Some key principles to remember when decluttering

1. It gets worse before it gets easier

Every single time I do a declutter – and I've done dozens over the years – I hit a point midway through where I'm sitting on the floor surrounded by papers, boxes, half-emptied shelves, rubbish bags and any number of other items of junk. I gaze at the disaster zone around me and question why I ever thought it would be a good idea to undertake this task in the first place.

There is a definitive point in every declutter where it looks decidedly worse than better. However, take heart my friend! The turning point is just ahead of you. Take a deep breath, remind yourself of how great it'll feel when all the crap is cleared and tackle the next pile.

2. It's not much fun

I don't know anyone – other than absolute pros like Marie Kondo herself – who would *choose* to spend their weekend decluttering over other options like long lunches, movie trips and binge-watching Netflix. I certainly wouldn't!

Decluttering does not come easily to me. As I mentioned earlier, the only reason I finally tackled my home office is that I knew this book wouldn't get written among the detritus around me.

You'll know your own motivations for finally getting rid of the stuff around you – whether it's reading this chapter, a big life change about to happen or a house move coming up. Don't feel like a weirdo if you're not jumping with excitement to get started – it's a big task, especially if you're doing it properly.

3. It takes a tonne of energy

Decluttering is *exhausting*, and not just physically with all the lifting, moving, bending down and stretching overhead. It's also mentally tiring, as you're making constant decisions about what stays, what goes and what will live where going forward. It might also be emotionally draining as you go through old mementos and papers; certain garments might even bring back happy or sad memories.

Don't be surprised if you're tired while going through the process – especially if you tackle your entire home over a day or two. When we did our full Marie Kondo day, we started at 7 a.m. and finished at 7 p.m. I was also twenty weeks pregnant! By chance, we had lots of leftovers in the fridge so we had frequent fuel-up breaks and a chance to sit down for ten minutes.

Have some nice snacks ready to go, order in food so you can maintain your focus, and have a breather every couple of hours.

4. Give yourself the evening/night off

I suggest you don't make social plans or other commitments for the evening/night after your declutter, for a couple of reasons.

One: it's incredibly annoying to have to abandon a declutter when you've got the finish line in sight – and it's very difficult to pick up where you left off the next day. The CBF (Can't Be Fucked) barometer is pretty high once you step away from the decluttering task, and you'll need to dig deep to get the motivation cranking again.

Two: refer to point 3 – you're likely to be zonked and the only thing you'll want to do is crash out on the sofa with a takeaway pizza and a very big glass of wine. In fact, why not set that as a reward for getting all your hard work done?

5. It's likely to create more work

Every declutter throws up papers that need to be filed, boring admin that needs to be completed and items that need to be repaired or returned.

Collate everything that requires action into one area and capture each action on a list. Once the declutter is completed, you can transfer these actions in order of priority onto your to-do list and tick through them quickly and efficiently.

When I tidied my home office, the resulting action list ran like this:

- sign and post two mail redirection forms
- pay an ASIC bill
- call our insurance provider and pay for the business workers' compensation insurance
- scan in a letter that had come to our mailbox and send to our real estate agent
- claim the Medicare refund for a medical scan
- book two spa treatments (I had found two gift vouchers for two different spas that would expire if I didn't use them).

Combined, these tasks were a lot more daunting when they lived as a jumbled mess of papers stuffed down the back of a shelf in my cupboard – rather than a neat stack of ten items accompanied by an action list in my notebook. I knocked all of them over in forty-five minutes and was extraordinarily proud of myself.

6. You may need to get others onboard

I'm sure many of you are living in homes with partners, kids or housemates (or sharing office space with colleagues) who you'll need to 'bring on the journey' of this decluttering adventure with you. After all, there's no point in you clearing all of your crap if theirs is still hanging in there for dear life – ruining any chance you have of domestic zen.

Getting them to read Marie's book would be a great starting point, or if that's a bridge too far you could condense the key points down for them (like I did with Wade).

I was amazed at his complete buy-in when we did our Epic Declutter – as it's not normally how he'd choose to invest his hard-earned Sunday. When I asked him about this, he said the fact that there was a system appealed and he could see progress as we tidied – and the fact that we did it together made it more fun.

A compelling incentive is a surefire way to get your fellow residents onboard – whether it's a new toy for young kids, new clothes for older kids, a date night for your partner or a case of wine for your roomies.

7. Get stuff out of the house ASAP

This is vital. I don't know about you, but I have a habit of putting together a bag of pre-loved items to go to Vinnies – which then sits next to the front door for weeks.

Try to allow time during your declutter day to complete a run to the charity shop and fill your wheelie bin, so that you avoid the pitfall of items boomeranging back into your home. By exiting old stuff immediately, you'll be able to enjoy the full energy shift that comes once everything is removed from your physical space.

The GRO list

1. Read *The Life-Changing Magic of Tidying Up* – it's a quick and simple read, and will give you a lot of motivation to get started.
2. Do an honest assessment of your home, office and car – is clutter an issue? Take the time to walk around them, opening cupboards and drawers as you go, to get an accurate picture of the clutter level.
3. Schedule a day within the next month to clear the crap.
4. Brief your support crew (AKA your fellow home dwellers) and negotiate any incentives required upfront.
5. Decide what your reward is going to be once you're done.
6. Clear your calendar the night before and the night after so you can be rested going into it and also have time to rest afterwards.
7. Make sure your bins are empty the week before so you have space to dump anything that's getting the red card.
8. Plan transport (if you don't have a car) to return items to friends or do a charity shop drop at the end of your declutter.

CHAPTER 3

Basics

Now that we have exited the excess 'stuff' from your life (can you feel the clear space?!), it's time to address some basics to help you on your way to getting remarkably organised.

Move from reactive to proactive mode

Many of us are spending significant amounts of our lives in reactive mode. We spend our days *reacting* to emails, requests, bosses, demands from kids, traffic, phone calls, social media notifications ... the list goes on and on.

It gets to the end of the day and you feel you haven't achieved a single thing that *you* wanted to achieve, and wonder how the hell you're going to get through the massive to-do list you have looming ahead of you.

This book is geared towards helping you move from reactive mode to proactive mode – firmly placing you back in the driving seat of your life. For a lot of you, this will be a pretty big paradigm shift as the habits of running reactively are so deeply entrenched.

In *The Seven Habits of Highly Effective People*, the first habit that author Stephen Covey identifies is 'Be Proactive'. In his opinion, operating as a proactive person is the flagstone of every other habit that follows.

He writes: '[Proactivity] is more than merely taking initiative. It means that, as human beings, we are responsible for our own lives. Our behaviour is a function of our decisions, not our conditions. We have the initiative and the responsibility to make things happen.'

He goes on to explain that highly proactive people embed this throughout their lives – they're in the driving seat.

In contrast, reactive people see themselves as being at the mercy of external stimuli – events, people, circumstances.

It would be a worthwhile exercise to observe the extent to which you feel your daily life is being governed by external factors that then require you to react to them.

> Making the switch from being reactive to proactive is one of the biggest leaps forward you can take when it comes to getting remarkably organised. And like most big leaps, it starts with some teeny-tiny steps.

As Covey writes: 'As we make and keep commitments, even small commitments, we begin to establish an inner integrity that gives us the awareness of self-control and the courage and strength to accept more of the responsibility for our own lives ... The power to make and keep commitments to ourselves is the essence of developing habits in effectiveness.'[1]

Making a small commitment to ourselves – be that getting up ten minutes earlier, making our bed or going for a walk – and executing that commitment every day is the holy grail of moving from reactive to proactive mode.

Work on your self-talk

How we speak to ourselves is incredibly powerful. In fact, I doubt we would ever speak to another person using the same tone and language we sometimes use to address ourselves. Imagine saying 'You're useless!' to your child. Or 'Why can't you just GET this?' to your team member. Or 'You're such a fucking idiot' to your best friend. Yet we speak to ourselves like this all day long.

Japanese author and researcher Masaru Emoto created the infamous water crystal experiments – taking pure water from lakes and streams and treating samples in different ways.

In a nutshell, the water that was subjected to positive, kind and loving words developed beautiful, symmetrical and hexagonal crystals. Water that was spoken to harshly or cruelly morphed into disfigured crystals. The upshot? Words have a lot of power.

Given that our bodies are approximately 60 per cent water, this study has enormous implications for the power of our self-talk.

Author Danielle LaPorte performed her own experiment using an apple and got her young son to help. They split an apple in two and put each half into its own sealed glass jar.

Every time they passed one half, the Apple of Positivity, they would tell it how fabulous it was:

'You're awesome!'

'You are perfect, gorgeous, useful.'

'We love you, apple!'

And the other half, the poor Apple of Negativity, got the opposite:

'Apple! You super suck! You no good, ugly, stinking piece of usefulness fruit.'

The results were staggering. After a month, the Apple of Positivity was in pretty good nick, with only one brown spot. In stark contrast, the Apple of Negativity was misshapen, rotten throughout and had been consumed by mould.

A friend of mine went through a phase of feeling all over the place after the birth of her first baby – something I now know firsthand is perfectly normal as you adjust to the chaos that a tiny human brings into your life. For almost a year afterwards, when she forgot to reply to a text or some other trivial thing, she would exclaim at how disorganised/forgetful/hopeless she was. Every time she told me this, I wondered at how her self-talk loop was running in her brain.

If you're telling yourself all day long how shockingly disorganised a human you are, do you think you're actually going to feel organised? Of course you're not – you're going to feel exactly how you're telling yourself you feel!

Many of you reading may be running an old tape that goes something along these lines:

'I'm hopelessly disorganised.'

'I'll never get on top of everything.'

'I can try some of the stuff in this book, but realistically
    I'm beyond help.'
'I'm just not an organised person.'

I can guarantee you right now that if that's how you're talking to yourself, that's exactly the situation in which you're going to find yourself.

As Henry Ford said: 'Whether you think you can or whether you think you can't, you're right.'

I challenge you over the days and weeks that we spend together during this book to act like a private investigator of your own thoughts. Notice how you're addressing yourself when it comes to organising your life, productivity and general life management. Are you your own biggest cheerleader or your biggest critic?

If you find that you *are* being rather tough on yourself, start to write some new language for yourself. You probably won't turn into a Type A Organised Person overnight; however, I can guarantee you that the pages of this book will give you bucketloads of small, actionable steps that you can start straight away.

Congratulate yourself on the small positive steps you take towards getting more in control of your life and remember that small steps add up to big steps over time.

It is vital that throughout the process of getting organised, you move not just into the physical driving seat (by taking the steps that I and others in the book suggest) but also the psychological driving seat – and the magic key to that is managing your self-talk carefully.

Getting rid of the stones in your shoes

You know how it feels when you have a little stone rattling around in your shoe. You start walking and notice it. You don't stop walking, as you figure you can deal with it. You keep walking and keep noticing it. It's definitely there. It's definitely not going away. You can put up with it, no biggie. You keep walking some more. Keep noticing it some more. Finally you stop and remove the stone as it's *so bloody annoying!* Then you get on with going wherever you need to be.

We are extraordinarily good at ignoring little stones in our shoes when it comes to life overall. They're the little niggly things that cause minor discomfort or inconvenience, but fly just below the radar so they don't quite merit us putting some time and energy into resolving them.

We grow used to dealing with them, so the irritation they cause levels off at a certain point. It's still there, though – we've just become comfortable with it.

I'll give you a couple of examples of the stones I have in my shoe right now.

One: As I already mentioned, we moved into this house three months ago and I finally got my home office in order recently. There is one last task that needs to be done, though, and that's getting the various framed photos, paintings and certificates up on the damn walls. Right now they are propped up against the wall, and I move them around as and when I need access to a particular cupboard.

The block to me ridding myself of this stone in my shoe is that they are currently in different types of frames – some in wood, some in black, some in white and some in metal.

I've decided I want them all to be consistent in white wooden frames, which means getting some reframed.

I should also note that my wonderful assistant has gone and bought said frames – I just need to get my ass in gear and match them up with the item to be framed so we can hang them.

Two: I moved my smartphone calendar over from iCal to Google Calendar … ooh about three years ago now. No matter how many times I have cleared iCal, tried to sync my phone or deleted old diary entries, I still get occasional reminders for a recurring appointment or meeting I haven't had for four or five years. Every time it happens, I look at my phone and get a little buzz of annoyance – then move on with my day, until it happens again.

There are a few big problems associated with having stones in our shoes.

We could be incredibly organised in every area of our lives, but these little niggly things tell us that we're actually an utterly disorganised human and we cheat ourselves out of the sense of accomplishment that comes from being on top of things.

They also – in tiny increments of time – build frustration and annoyance into our days, which is completely unnecessary and quite frankly something we could all do without. If I were to calculate the combined minutes that I've spent being frustrated at each of these stones in my shoe, I think I would get quite a fright.

Probably the most irritating thing, though, about having stones in our shoes is that they're generally extremely easy to resolve!

We're not talking a major logistics operation to get some frames on the wall, or go into a store and get my phone sorted out (when I think of how many times I've walked past an Apple store, gah!). It's just that other more pressing – and complicated – tasks arise that seem to need our more urgent attention.

> We are all always going to have stones in our shoes; the trick is to exit them out of our lives as soon as we can, so we can buy back that mental energy to devote to more productive things.

A blogger I know, Beth Macdonald, took a great approach to dealing with the various stones in her shoe. She wrote a list of all those niggly little jobs that had been sticking around for years (in some cases), and set herself a goal of tackling just one a week. They varied between having the carpets in her house steam-cleaned to hanging a mirror that had been waiting to be hung for seven years. Slow and steady – I love this approach!

Take a moment to list the stones you currently have rattling around in your shoe – it's not a pleasant exercise, I know, but capturing them on a list is the first step to getting them sorted.

Next, identify the three key steps you need to do in order to get rid of that stone. Is there someone you need to help you? Do you need to buy something that will enable you to complete that task? Do you need to take an item somewhere to have it fixed?

When I apply this to my frames situation, it looks like this:

1. Pull out all the things to be framed along with the empty frames, and match them up together.

2. Identify what still needs a frame or needs to be professionally framed.
3. Brief my assistant to organise remaining frames.

From here, there are still a couple of steps to complete:

4. Book someone to come hang the frames.
5. Tell them where to hang them.

The beauty of dealing with tasks by looking at the immediate next three steps is that they break the inertia with which we've been approaching (or rather, not approaching) them to date and we get some momentum going. It breaks the back of the task so that we can complete the rest of it with relative ease.

I fully realise that I have secured myself potentially thousands of accountability buddies in revealing these two stones in my shoe – so I have set myself a goal of resolving them before I finish writing this chapter. Feel free to check in on me to make sure I've done them ...

Get good sleep

Another cornerstone of getting remarkably organised is to aim to get good sleep each night. There is a direct correlation between how organised I'm feeling about my life at any one time and how rested I am.

I was shocked to read that between 20 and 30 per cent of road deaths in Australia are caused by driver fatigue,[2] almost as many as those caused by drunk drivers.

Now I know that getting your life in order is nowhere near as critical as accidents like these. I do, however, think we can draw some comparisons between steering our lives when we're feeling generally rested/with-it, and steering them when we're feeling flat-out exhausted.

When we've had a good night's sleep, motivation is high, we are more efficient with our time and we're more likely to feel like we're in the driver's seat.

When we've had a crappy night's sleep, or a run of poor sleeping, the Can't Be Fucked Index is high and everything just feels that bit more difficult. All we can think of is getting a chance to rest, and our Future Selves are the last thing we're concerned about. It's as if we're operating in survival mode.

The Transport Accident Commission estimates that if a driver falls asleep for just four seconds while travelling at a speed of 100 kilometres per hour, the car will have gone 111 metres without a driver in control.[3] Four seconds!

If we compare this to being organised in our lives, the constant course corrections required when we're operating at less than our maximum capacity steal valuable time and energy from the key tasks at hand.

Now I know that getting your required zzz's each night is going to be more achievable for some of us than others; children, partners, working hours and sleep issues can prevent us from springing out of bed each morning full of the joys that a restful sleep brings. As I write this chapter, I'm anticipating the arrival of our first baby – and I know that the nights of seven to nine hours of uninterrupted sleep will feel like a magical fantasy in a few short weeks!

As part of laying the foundations for getting more in control of your life, I strongly suggest that you consider the element of sleep. Are you getting enough rest? Or is everyday fatigue slowing you down and preventing you from being the on-the-ball superhuman you know you're capable of being?

Get some nice kit

I am a self-confessed stationery nut. I adore my planners, to-do lists and assorted little notepads that live in different areas in the house and office. kikki.K and Typo are where you'll find me in my element, and I've even created some of my own stationery to meet the needs I had to get my life more organised.

Having a few key pieces of kit around me makes me feel like I'm on top of things – it's that simple. It brings me great joy to sit down to a year/month/week/day planning sesh with some smart and pleasant-on-the-eye stationery to help me on my way.

I also have a beautiful monogrammed notebook and a fancy pen that was a gift from Wade to celebrate a special speaking gig a few years ago. With my stationery, notebook, pen and phone (also replete with monogrammed cover), I feel I *look* the part of being organised – and somehow it helps me actually *be* more organised. I liken it to having some hot new activewear – I always feel like I do better in a yoga class when I'm wearing a new colour-coordinated outfit!

In the spirit of not attracting more clutter, I've learned over the years which essential pieces of stationery kit truly work for me. To have a plethora of bulky ring binders, storage containers, desk organisers, coloured pens and various iterations of notepads would have the opposite outcome. Superfluous 'stuff' would make me feel less rather than more organised.

My essential stationery kit consists of:

- a pad of the daily to-do list structure I developed and use every day (we'll chat more about this in Chapter 9)
- a weekly meal planner
- a Weekly Habits Scorecard (more on this in Chapter 5)
- an A5 notebook
- my fancy pen
- a notepad for random lists/ideas in the kitchen and in my home office.

For me, it's all about quality over quantity.

Invest in something that will help you feel more organised as we embark on this journey together. It might be a weekly planner, a beautiful new pen or a new folder. You might be more tech-led than me – so for you it might mean upgrading your phone or some clever apps.

Having an item that has a daily presence in your life to remind you of your mission to get more organised – and that will also spark joy (in our dear friend Marie's words) – will be a symbolic and very helpful little reminder to keep you on track.

Have an inspiring space in which to work

We have already explored the concept of the Epic Declutter in the previous chapter; however, it goes without saying that this should extend to your workspace as well. The goal is to have a clear, constructive space where you feel that you can do your best thinking or work.

In *Die Empty*, Todd Henry writes about the idea of a 'bliss station' – a place that you can go to create your life's work. For him, the opportunity came when he and his wife were working on a renovation of their home and there was a small space at the back of the new garage where he could set up a desk.

For me, it came when we moved into this house and I (pinch me!) got to create a whole room that inspired me to do great work. It's decidedly girlier than the rest of the house and is decorated with blues, greys and dusty pink.

Around me are my favourite books, photos of the special people and moments in my life, a salt lamp, candles and an essential oil diffuser. I try to have a small bunch of fresh flowers on my desk and line up the thank-you notes I receive from people along the mantelpiece.

It is *heavenly* to work from and I feel lucky every time I get to spend a day in here, writing, planning or having calls with my team and mentees.

My desk is deliberately clear of any items that aren't going to help me achieve what's on my to-do list. To give you an idea, the inventory as I write in this moment looks like this:

- computer
- keyboard
- mouse
- salt lamp
- fresh flowers
- my to-do list notepad
- phone
- phone headphones
- pen
- notebook
- lip balm

- my meal planner (as that's a to-do list item today)
- a medical referral form (also on today's to-do list).

All my other work items are stored out of sight in the cupboard.

For example, I have a separate notebook for the monthly sessions I do with my mentees. I had a call at 9 a.m. this morning with one of them – Cathy – and once the call was finished, I put the mentoring notebook back in the cupboard.

Ditto for random office supplies that I need only once a week or so, like a stapler, post-its and stamps. Previously, I had a box of kit from my office desk that I thought I would *absolutely need* on my desk at home as well. Those very items were still living in an unopened box three months later, and it really made me question how much I actually needed them crowding my workspace. None of it needs to be readily accessible, so it can live out of sight for the vast majority of the time and not take up valuable visible (and therefore mental) space.

The insane luxury of having my own room at home is not wasted on me, and it's something that I have wanted for a very long time. You may not be in a position to have a full room right now; however, a bliss station is just that – an area for you to do your work.

This could take the form of a corner nook with a great chair and collapsible desk, a box of kit that you unpack onto the dining table when you need to get some focus time, or simply zhooshing your desk at work to make it a clearer, more productive space.

Trying to get your shit together while surrounded by clutter, ugly things and non-essential items is not giving you your best shot at success.

Many successful people attest to the 'tidy desk, tidy mind' philosophy. Craig Newmark, founder of Craigslist, keeps a super-minimalist desk – he has one big screen connected to a desktop computer and a phone. That's it.

Michael Moritz, chairman at Sequoia Capital, describes his desk: 'Two computers, a mobile phone (no desk phone needed), a small bottle of whiskey for the bad surprise, a stash of dark chocolate (82% cocoa) for twice-daily medication, a bottle of Pellegrino water and a pair of analogue clocks as a reminder that our business is about art as well as science.'[4]

Having a space that you love to think, plan and work creates a powerful anchor to getting more organised – even if that's one end of the tidied-up kitchen bench with a gorgeous-smelling candle lit on it! Think of it as an oasis of clarity as you strive to extend that clarity across the whole spectrum of your life.

The GRO list

1. Complete the Organisational Wheel exercise in the next chapter to identify the areas of your life that are most in need of getting remarkably organised.
2. Make a list of any stones in your shoe that you can spot right now – naming them is the hardest part, I promise!
3. Transfer one of these stones per week onto your to-do list. Remember slow and steady is the best approach here.

4. Honestly ask yourself how well you are sleeping right now. Start one daily habit that's geared towards helping you get more sleep, and see whether that helps. (More on habits in Chapter 5.)
5. Invest in a nice thing or two that will help you as you get remarkably organised – something you'll get to use every day that will make you feel happy.
6. Identify where and what your bliss station might look like, and spend some time doing what you need to make it blissful. It might be decluttering, tidying or injecting some inspirational items into it.

CHAPTER 4

Priorities and standards

Let's talk about the key priorities in your life.

The dictionary definition of 'priority' is: *something given special attention.*

Even if you don't think you prioritise, you already do. An article on Fast Company made an interesting point – our calendars never lie. So we might say to ourselves that family is our number-one priority, but we schedule a meeting for 6 p.m ... Therefore prioritising business over family.[1]

I firmly believe that a major pitfall for most of us in trying to be more organised is that we place everything on an equal footing in our lives. We believe that everything needs special attention – therefore everything is a priority!

So really, we have no priorities as everything is a priority – how's that for a brain twister?!

If everything is a priority, nothing is a priority.

This results in the crazy-making feeling that everything is equally important and we can't get ahead in any particular area.

When I ask people what the biggest block is for them in feeling more organised, they will often say 'overwhelm' – that every area of their lives feels disorganised and they feel they're constantly juggling (unsuccessfully) to get each of those areas under control.

It is impossible to give every area of your life special attention.

I'll say that again: it is impossible to give every area of your life special attention.

I'm not saying that we should neglect some areas. I'm saying that we need to accept that we're not, in fact, superhuman. If we want to see solid results in a specific area, then that means giving that area some concentrated focus – at least for a short period of time.

This is especially relevant when we're going on this getting remarkably organised journey together.

As writer Johann Wolfgang von Goethe once said, 'Things which matter most must never be at the mercy of things which matter least.'

Identifying your priorities

In my first book, *Remarkability*, I created a Wheel of Life exercise that helped measure how happy you are with the different areas of your life. It's a super-simple graphic tool that delivers some pretty hefty insights. I'll explain.

The only reason a wheel works is that it can roll along the ground. If you have flat or uneven edges to the wheel, it's not going to roll anymore. This is why this exercise is so valuable – as you can see in an instant where the uneven edges are in your life. These edges represent a block, which is directly affecting all the other areas of your life – preventing you from rolling smoothly along the ground. If you're not rolling smoothly, you're feeling stressed, overwhelmed, guilty and probably rather frustrated.

I've created a similar tool to help you, at this point, to identify what areas are in most need of special attention in your life when it comes to getting remarkably organised.

Most of us will have the following key commitments in our lives:

- career/business
- home
- partner
- family
- friends
- finances
- life admin (mail, insurance, etc.)
- health (exercise, sleep)
- food
- car.

However, you may have extra categories (hobbies, community activities, second businesses). You might also have sub-categories within categories – for example, exercise might be a key element for you. So that you can personalise your Organisational Wheel to your life, I've added two blank areas in the graphic too.

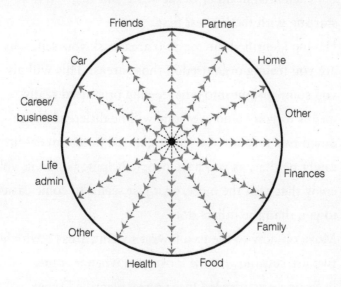

Friends

Partner

Car

Home

Career/
business

Other

Life
admin

Finances

Other

Family

Health

Food

ORGANISATIONAL WHEEL

You can also download a free worksheet to do this exercise from the store on my website – lorrainemurphy.com.au.

Here's what you do:

1. Once you're ready to go, think about each area one by one. How organised do you feel out of 10 in that specific area? Allocate a score out of 10 to it. Then draw a line across that number in that section of the circle. Once you have completed all 12 areas, you should have the rough outline of a wheel.

2. When each of these areas is plotted on a diagram like the one above, you essentially have a scorecard with which to evaluate how organised the various areas of your life are right now.

3. Put each area in order of the score you've given it – starting with the highest first.

4. Having identified the top two areas, ask yourself: why are you feeling organised in those areas? This will give you some insight into what feeling organised really means to *you* – and everyone will be different. Write down two reasons you feel organised in that area – it might be that, as you have people helping you in it, you enjoy that area the most, or it just seems to come easier to you than the others do.

5. Move on now to the two lowest scoring areas – which two are causing you the most pain when it comes to feeling organised? Once you've identified them, write down two things that would help you feel more organised in those areas. If you have a number of different areas ranked the same, then choose the two that you think are having the most negative impact on your life overall and work with them.

From this exercise, you should have a clear picture of what areas you should give priority to as you work through this book. If you have a handful of areas – or even one area – that you *do* feel organised in, let's leave that to do its thing for the moment while we tackle the more problematic areas together.

If you did this exercise and realised that you feel disorganised in *every* area of your life, please don't worry. That's why we're going through this process together!

Some firm words on standards ...

I attended a weekend seminar with the inimitable Tony Robbins a few years ago. Alongside the many 'aha' moments I had over the three and a half days, there was one thing he said that especially resonated with me.

Tony said that the source of all unhappiness is when the mental 'blueprint' we have for how life should be does not match up with the reality we're experiencing.

So we feel unhappy with our partner when they're not the ideal partner we have visualised. We feel unhappy when our team is not producing the kind of work we can see in our mind's eye. We feel unhappy when our house is a mess and the image we have in our heads is a pristine, sparkling space.

It all comes down to standards.

Every single one of us has a standards blueprint that is unique to us. Partners may have different standards about what constitutes a tidy and clean home (hello, arguments!), or colleagues might have varying standards on how thorough a client presentation needs to be.

We will also have different standards for the different areas of our lives. For example, Person A might have very high standards for their career, but their health standards are relatively low. Person B might have inordinately high standards for how their home looks or is run, yet the food they eat could be of negligible importance as they don't have a high standard for that area.

The unique standards DNA that we each have inbuilt is like a fingerprint – it's as individual as we are. You may have high standards in a specific area of your life, whereas my standards are super-low in that very same area.

When I speak to people who are struggling to be more organised in their lives, a common theme seems to arise. They may be trying to prioritise several things at once (refer to the previous section); however, they can also have unrealistically high standards within each – or maybe even all – of those areas.

This makes us crazy.

> You will send yourself around the freaking twist if you try to achieve and then maintain high standards in every single area of your life.

As well as knowing what priorities you should have (based on our previous exercise), you should also understand where your standards sit in each of the life areas we have identified.

For example, I can tell you quite easily that my standards break down is as follows:

High standards

- career/business
- family
- home
- food

I apply probably the highest standards to my business at this point in my life. I also strive to have a happy, loving relationship with Wade and Lexi. Having a clean and clear home is important to me as it gives me mental clarity – as well as looking nice! Eating fresh, healthful food is the most important way for me to stay healthy and I invest a lot of money, time and focus into eating as well as I can.

Medium standards
- health
- extended family
- friendships

I stay fit by doing four or five exercise sessions a week, but I don't have a grand plan to complete a triathlon, take on uber-yogi status or obsess over daily Fitbit reports. If I'm enjoying my exercise and feeling reasonably fit and strong, then I'm happy.

I am also the first to identify that I don't have hugely high standards when it comes to investing in my friendships. I have a small group of people (friends and family) who I am close to and with whom I try to stay in as regular contact as possible; however, I've had to accept that being the perfect friend/daughter/sister is not achievable with everything else I want to get done on a day-to-day basis.

Low standards
- finance
- car
- personal admin

I obviously strive for an abundance of money – I imagine most people do. When I say my standards for finance are low, I mean that I don't expend huge energy on a regular basis tracking and tinkering with my personal finances.

The monthly running of my finances is set up quite autonomously – I simply do not have the time nor the care factor to do anything more. I figure if the essential infrastructure is in place and I'm driving my opportunities to earn income as much as I can, then it will look after itself.

I do not care to track my spending, do monthly budget reconciliations or go any further in depth than I absolutely need to. I know how much comes into my personal transaction account each month for spending, and I can't remember the last time I overspent from that account.

I don't weight personal admin very highly, either. If it comes down to the wire, I am happy to drop the ball with health insurance claims and the like in order to have higher standards in other areas of my life.

For example, as soon as we moved house Wade spent a few hours calling, emailing and filling out online forms to change the address on his driver's licence, bank accounts, insurance policies and so on. I didn't, and still haven't. Instead I put a mail redirection on our old address and figure I'll get to changing everything over at some stage.

I knew that Richard Branson was a pretty active guy from what I had read about him; however, when I had the opportunity to spend a week on Necker Island (his private island) last year, I saw first-hand how much of a high standard he holds himself to when it comes to physical activity.

Every morning – probably before most of us had crawled out of our beds – Richard played tennis, kitesurfed, swam or did something else to keep himself fit. It was clear to me that physical exercise was a non-negotiable for him and as a result he started every day by focusing on that area of his life.

Identifying our standards across the different areas of our lives can be incredibly helpful, for a few different reasons:

1. It helps us shed light on why certain situations especially piss us off – particularly when what we want doesn't match up with what we get.
2. It gives us an insight into where conflicts might occur with others.
3. It helps us navigate what compromises we may need to create to make ourselves and others happy – for example, if you have very high standards for both your career and your sleep, is there a happy medium you need to find so that your long work hours don't mean you miss out on rest?
4. It also makes us more effective in eliminating unhealthy patterns in our lives. Neuroscientist Elliot Berkman states: 'People who want to kick their habit for reasons that are aligned with their personal values will change their behaviour faster than people who are doing it for external reasons such as pressure from others.'[2]

High standards? Then suck it up

If you're going to set high standards in multiple areas, then be prepared to own that and pump extra energy into those areas.

As I already mentioned, eating and enjoying healthy food is one of the areas in my life for which I set a very high standard. It's vitally important to me to eat as well as I possibly can, at least 80 per cent of the time.

This means I do a weekly meal plan, shop for my own food across three different stores, bring my food into the office every day (unless I've got breakfast or lunch meetings), cook dinners from scratch most nights, and take the time to sit down with no other distractions to enjoy my meals in peace and quiet.

Achieving this self-imposed standard means that on average each week I spend twenty-two hours on food alone! This includes the planning, shopping, prepping and eating over seven days.

I have days often (okay, very often!) when I wish I was someone who would be happy to order their groceries online, grab a coffee and croissant en route to the office as their breakfast, eat a takeaway sandwich while walking between meetings or order takeaway a few nights a week. It also sounds so blissfully *easy*! And think of the time I'd save!!!

However, I know that it simply wouldn't work for me, so when I'm complaining to myself about having to make green smoothies, lunch and snacks at 9 p.m. for the next day – I tell myself that I'm the one choosing to have these standards, and to suck it up, sister. If they are the standards I want in my life, I need to work to make them a reality.

The concept of 'satisficing'

You might be a little taken aback when I make a little confession to you now.

I am not someone who obsesses over the fine details, who looks at four different ways a task can be approached, who spends hours and hours rehearsing a big talk, who goes over an event schedule a dozen times until it's 'just so'.

In fact, for a very long time I thought I was just lazy! That is, until I came across the concept of 'satisficing' at an event a few years ago, and rushed back excitedly to the team to share it with them.

The word 'satisficing' is a mash-up between 'satisfy' and 'suffice', which was created by political scientist/economist/ sociologist/psychologist/computer scientist (how's that for a skillset?), Herbert Simon. The more formal name for his theory is 'bounded rationality', but apparently Simon himself preferred the more lay term 'satisficing'.

Simon explained that people do not set out to get maximum benefit from a certain course of action, as they can't mentally deal with the expanse of information that would be needed to do that. The human mind puts a necessary restriction on itself, what Simon calls 'cognitive limits'.

He described two different kinds of people: economic and administrative. The economic person seeks to maximise, by seeking out the best alternative among those available to them. In contrast, the administrative person efficiently looks for the course of action that is 'good enough'.[3]

I realised that I am the 'administrative person' in this theory. I will generally find the solution that works best and fastest when undertaking a task, which can often mean I'll complete something quicker than someone who has more of an 'economic man (or woman)' mindset would.

Or maybe I *am* just really lazy!

Done is better than perfect

Another mantra of which I constantly remind myself and my team is that 'done is better than perfect'. So often we tweak, tweak and tweak a little more, telling ourselves that whatever the task is – be it a client presentation, tidying the house or finding a new fridge – it's just not quite right yet. We are actually delaying ourselves from a) completing the damn task and b) moving on to the next task!

> Accepting that not everything needs to be absolutely perfect will help you no end on your journey to getting more organised.

If you are a hardcore perfectionist, have a play with getting your next task to 'satisficing' standard rather than 'perfect'. As you practise more and more, you'll flex your 'satisficing' muscle and it will become easier over time.

You are never going to get everything done

Wade and I went through a phase of having this conversation after our respective days at the office. It would go something like this:

> Him: 'So how was your day?'
> Me: 'Great – we had a very positive meeting with this client, the team is on fire and I ticked off my whole to-do list.'
> Him: 'You did your ENTIRE to-do list?'
> Me: 'Umm ... yes.'
> Him: 'How the fuck did you do that?'

We went for *weeks* having these conversations, until I finally asked him why he thought it was so weird that I would be able to tick off the various items on my to-do list most days.

It turned out he thought I was talking about my *overall* to-do list – that is, all the things I have to do over the next day/

week/month, whereas what I meant was my to-do list for that particular day. Confusion cleared.

'OF COURSE I don't do my entire to-do list,' I told him laughing. 'That's impossible!'

And I meant that.

> We will never, ever get to the bottom of the bulging to-do list that most of us have – either in list format somewhere or buzzing around our brains. To think otherwise is to pursue an impossible dream.

In Oprah's *What I Know for Sure*, there's a phrase that hit me like a hammer in the heart when I read it. It goes: 'One day when in the final analysis of our lives – when the to-do lists are no more, when the frenzy is finished, when our email inboxes are empty – the only thing that will have any lasting value is whether we've loved others and whether they've loved us.'[4]

The thought of one day not having a to-do list shocked me to the core – and I realised that everyone, no matter what stage of life they're at, has *something* that they need to do – whether it's phoning a friend, putting that last load of laundry on or watching that TV show.

Accepting that one day I won't have a to-do list anymore, and therefore it's actually okay to not get every single thing done every day, was an extremely liberating thought for me.

We'll talk a lot more about to-do lists in Chapter 9, but for now let's all spend a moment absorbing that thought: We will never, ever get absolutely everything done.

And that's perfectly okay.

The GRO list

1. Using my template, identify the key areas in your life and complete the Organisational Wheel with those areas in mind.
2. Consider these various areas of your life, and – being very honest with yourself – assign a standard to each of them (high, medium, low).
3. If you do have high standards in an area, accept that the area will require more time and energy from you in order to meet those standards so you feel happy with it.
4. Think about how you could 'satisfice' some tasks in your life rather than 'perfect' them. Test the concept and see whether it helps you complete tasks faster.
5. Accept that you are never, ever going to get everything done. I mean it.

CHAPTER 5

The power of routine

Every single one of us has routines in our life, be they beneficial, detrimental, big, small, regular or irregular.

Even if you don't consider yourself as a 'routine person', I can guarantee you if we spent some time together we would be able to identify little routines that you practise.

It might be ordering the same coffee at the same café from Monday to Friday at some time between 8.25 a.m. and 8.50 a.m.

It might be checking your Facebook newsfeed when waiting for the kids at school pick-up.

It might be never taking the top newspaper from the stack at the newsagent and instead taking the second one.

It might be catching the train with the same friend most Thursday mornings.

We all have these routines, which are baked into our lives – often so much so that we don't even notice them anymore.

The interesting thing about routines is that they enable us to switch into mental autopilot.

Assuming you know how to drive, cast your mind back to when you were just learning ...

You would sit in the car, carefully fasten your seatbelt and insert the key in the ignition. Once the car was started, you would check all your mirrors were set up to your satisfaction, carefully test the accelerator, put the car into first gear (if, like me, you learnt on a manual), release the handbrake, then gently – oh so gently – push the accelerator down while simultaneously releasing the clutch. Then, if you were lucky first time, you would lurch off on your way.

Once you're moving, it's action stations.

You check all your mirrors in order – constantly. You are hyper-alert for what the drivers in front of you are doing, what that person behind you is doing (oh, there's a pedestrian – brake!), you're monitoring your speed, observing every road sign, and slowing down aaaages before your turn so you have plenty of time to put on your indicator and ease off the road.

Phew, wasn't it exhausting?!

It required every last fibre of your concentration to get the car started and move from A to B. You would arrive at your destination elated to have made it, and exhausted by the mental exertion of the whole thing.

Fast forward to now.

I bet you can navigate ten lane changes, have a heated debate with your front seat passenger, change the radio station twenty times, accommodate five drivers pulling out in front of you, plan your day in your head, monitor the kids in the back, make five phone calls, decide on your next holiday destination and spot a great new restaurant you must try – all in a thirty-minute car trip.

You don't *for a moment* think about what side of the steering wheel the indicator is on, whether you're in the right gear or if you checked your side mirror in the last five minutes.

I know I have set off for home in the car, only to find myself driving to our old house as the routine of getting there is so built into my brain. I imagine all drivers out there have had a similar experience.

We have spent so many hours driving that the entire process is completely automatic, meaning that our minds are free to focus on all the other things in our lives. Driving is a routine.

Let's consider this in the context of how we drive our lives, and the power of routine becomes patently obvious.

> When we have constructive routines built into our every day, it frees up unimaginable mental energy to devote to the 'big' stuff.

Stuff like making our goals a reality, investing time in our relationships with the people around us, and even the very valuable pastime of day-dreaming.

I love how Michael McCullough, a professor of psychology at the University of Miami, describes routines. He calls them 'mental butlers' – meaning that when we have them operating well in our lives, we save time and energy and reduce stress by skipping the mental back and forth of making a decision and kick directly into getting the task at hand done.

In *The Power of Habit*, author Charles Duhigg writes that an incredible 40 to 45 per cent of what we do every day feels like a decision, but is actually habit. Imagine how much more brain power we could buy back if we upped this by even 1 per cent?!

If we can hardwire positive routines into our lives, we are essentially buying back the opportunity to devote ourselves to the big stuff – meaning we achieve more, we are in charge of our lives and, most importantly, we feel happier.

The four levels of competence

At this point, you might be reading this and thinking, 'I have absolutely no routine in my life. I'm screwed.'

You're not.

You already have routines in your life, you may just not be aware of them – and they may not be serving you as well as they could.

Becoming aware of how competent we are when it comes to our routines is the first step in building productive daily rituals that will help us feel more organised and on top of life generally.

There are four levels of competence, which were articulated by Noel Burch of the Gordon Training Institute in the 1970s:

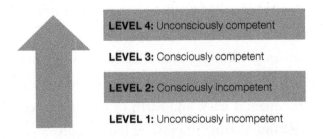

LEVEL 4: Unconsciously competent

LEVEL 3: Consciously competent

LEVEL 2: Consciously incompetent

LEVEL 1: Unconsciously incompetent

THE FOUR LEVELS OF COMPETENCE

Let's start at the bottom on Level 1, Unconsciously Incompetent. This is when we are not good at something and are blissfully unaware of the fact. In fact, we're feeling pretty good about life! Let's take the example of baking a loaf of bread – we assume if we *did* try to bake one, we'd turn out the perfect loaf first time. After all, how difficult can it be?

On Level 2, Consciously Incompetent, we realise that actually we're not doing so well on the baking front. This is likely to be the level at which we make the most mistakes. We might have tried to bake a loaf of bread but it collapsed as soon as it emerged from the oven, and our second attempt was still doughy in the middle. We now have a choice – do we want to get better at baking bread?

If we decide we *do* want to work on our newly desired skill, we begin to work on it. We watch some YouTube videos, consult some friends who can bake and commit to practising our bread-making skills. We gradually become competent at it – reaching Level 3. However, because we are Consciously Competent, we still need to apply significant concentration and effort each time we bake a loaf; we're a work in progress.

With ongoing practice, we don't need to think as much about what we're doing in order to successfully bake bread. For example, my grandmother baked a loaf of wholemeal soda bread every day for probably fifty years. Watching her bake was amazing.

Nothing was weighed, all the ingredients were measured by sight. She could maintain a full conversation the whole time she was baking, as well as completing various other tasks in the kitchen as she prepared the bread – tarts were made, dishes washed and the wood-burning stove kept topped up.

Even though she was hardly aware that she was making the bread, every loaf was perfect. I never once remember a loaf not turning out well. She was operating on Level 4. She had created the necessary neural pathways so that she could bake the daily bread with little or no active thought (refer back to the car driving example we talked about earlier). She was Unconsciously Competent.

My point here is that the first step to establishing productive routines in our lives is to realise that they would probably help us in some way, as it's affecting our lives not to have those routines running (Level 2).

We then take up the challenge of creating some routines and actively work on practising them (Level 3). I've lots more to help you on this coming up.

Once we have successfully practised the routine for long enough, it is embedded in our lives and we don't expend very much energy at all on making it happen (Level 4).

A routine is just a chain of habits

Embarking on a whole new routine is daunting to say the least. We feel we have to massively overhaul every area of our lives and overnight turn into this perfect person who has the perfect day. Every single fucking day.

We look at fitness models on Instagram talking about their morning routines and it feels a million miles from anything we ourselves might hope to achieve for one morning alone – never mind every single morning for the rest of our lives!

I find it helpful to change how I think about a routine from being a big daunting block of perfection to a set of smaller habits linked together in a chain.

It goes back to one of my favourite riddles:

Question: How do you eat an elephant?
Answer: One bite at a time.

What is a habit? *It's a sequence of actions regularly followed.*

Starting to see routines as conjoined baby steps of individual habits rather than one giant leap makes creating a routine feel a lot more achievable.

The science behind habits

The science around the forming of a new habit is fascinating, at least to me.

I first learned about it in my last year of high school when I was working at a sports retailer (I still have no idea how I did this job, being the least sporty person probably ever). We had a sales trainer come and train us on how to upsell to customers.

The goal was to increase the number of items that customers purchased to 2.5 items per sale; the idea being that by consistently focusing on that goal, the revenue of the stores would be significantly boosted.

As you can imagine, this sales trainer didn't have the easiest of tasks. Ninety per cent of the teams at the stores were aged 15–19 and working at the stores was more of a social engagement than anything.

For most of us, offering a customer an additional item was terrifying. We were school and university students, not 'salespeople', and we felt we would be seen as being pushy if we invited customers to buy anything other than the item they had originally come in for. It sat far beyond our comfort zone to try this new course of action.

The trainer explained that we could start small – for example, if a customer was buying new training shoes, we could casually ask if they needed some new sports socks. He also explained that everything is difficult the first time you do it, and the trick was to practise – over and over again.

It works like this: when we do something for the first time, it creates a brand-new neural pathway in our brains. The second time we do it, the pathway runs a tiny bit deeper, and then each time we complete that action it gets progressively more established. If we repeat that action enough, then the neural pathway becomes deep-etched into our brains – to the point where we don't have to think about it.

This is why riding a bike, driving a car or making our bowl of cereal in the morning is something we don't even have to consciously be aware that we're doing anymore. As we have repeated that action so many times, it is essentially engraved in our brains.

By explaining to us how our brains worked, the sales trainer succeeded in getting us to strike out and try a new behaviour – with the goal of repeating it over and over until we didn't need to think about it anymore.

And it worked. We hit the 2.5 items per customer target and maintained it for months afterwards.

Now, for the science bit ...

When we do something for the first time, it originates in the prefrontal cortex of our brains, which is right behind our forehead – and relative to our evolution, is one of the newest parts of our brain.

When we repeat that action several times (becoming a habit), it moves into the basal ganglia near the centre of our skull – one of the oldest parts of our brain. When behaviours originate in the basal ganglia, it doesn't feel like thought – it's automatic.

The science differs on how long it actually takes to form a new habit. Some experts claim it takes twenty-one days, others six weeks, and others even longer.

Psychologist and author of *Making Habits, Breaking Habits*, Jeremy Dean, coined the term 'automaticity' to describe when a habit or routine is properly ingrained. He found that the period of time required to hit the level of automaticity correlated with the difficulty of the new habit. So, for example, getting up five minutes earlier would be relatively easy (unless you reeeeally love your bed!), but getting up two hours earlier might prove more challenging.

His studies concluded that the average time taken among participants in his study to ingrain a new habit was sixty-six days.[1]

For me personally, if I keep something up for two weeks it's generally pretty ingrained – however, a break from the habit (due to travel, for example) would mean I'd need to quite actively re-establish it.

Forming strong habits

Author and journalist Charles Duhigg wrote an entire book on habits, titled *The Power of Habits*. In it, he explores in depth the elements of habit forming. He breaks the forming of a habit down into three core stages: the cue, the action and the reward.

Cue	▶	Action	▶	Reward

The cue is whatever triggers us to launch into our habit; the action (or number of actions) is the actual habit being performed; and the reward is the feeling or satisfaction we gain from completing the habit.

Let's look at a few examples:

Habit 1 – Making your morning coffee

Cue: Walking into the kitchen after you wake up.

Actions: Filling the water tank in the coffee machine, putting a coffee pod in the slot, taking a mug out of the cupboard, pressing the button.

Reward: A delicious hot mug of coffee to start your day.

Habit 2 – Going for a run

Cue: Walking to the front door and putting on your running shoes.

Action: Running around the park for thirty minutes.

Reward: Feeling energised and proud that you've completed your daily exercise.

Habit 3 – Writing your to-do list

Cue: Sitting down at your desk in the morning.

Actions: Consulting diary for the day, looking at items from yesterday's list that haven't been completed, writing to-do list items for the day ahead.

Reward: Feeling you have a clear plan for the day.

The key to establishing a strong habit is to ensure that all three elements are present. So there's a clear *cue* to start that habit, a defined *action* that needs to happen and a *reward* associated once the action has been completed.

I'll give you an example from my own life.

I wasn't really the bed-making type of person. I'd throw back the covers when I got up in the morning and start my day, then throw them back over me when I got into bed that night. I decided that I did, in fact, want to be the bed-making type, and actively tried to make my bed every morning for a few weeks. Now it's something I don't even think about – and I would say our bed goes unmade maybe one day a month.

Making the bed (if Wade hasn't already made it) is the last thing I do before I leave our bedroom in the morning.

I'm dressed, my hair and make-up are done, and I have assembled a pile of things I need to take with me for the day ahead. The moment before I step out of the bedroom is my cue to make the bed.

The actions I take are to put the extra pillows back on the bed, stretch the sheets and blanket back and tuck them under the mattress, fold the duvet up over the bed and arrange the cushions on top.

The reward for me is walking out the door feeling like my shit is together, and a second reward hits when I walk back into our bedroom that night and it's a tidy, welcoming space.

The trick in forming new habits, I believe, is making sure that the relevant cues are in place to prompt you to take action, and that there is an adequate reward at the end of it.

One of my past team members, Emily, had a genius cue to get herself out the door to the gym. On cold winter mornings, the last thing she felt like doing was stepping out into the dark outdoors to haul her ass to do some intense cardio. A tactic she developed was to sleep in her (clean, thankfully) gym gear, so that when she woke up in the morning her cue was that she was already dressed, so she should get moving.

If you don't gain enough satisfaction from successfully completing your habit, then self-incentivising as a means to a reward works beautifully – more about this shortly in 'Give yourself gold stars' on page 72.

Layering habits to form a routine

Once you start to break your desired routines down into individual habits, it becomes a lot easier to build that overall routine.

I believe that the best way to form a new routine is to gradually *layer* individual habits on top of each other – almost like creating a very organised layer cake!

If you try to undertake a whole new routine in one hit, you are setting yourself a very high benchmark for success – especially if you don't have any routine in place yet.

Starting with one element of the routine, mastering that (or becoming Unconsciously Competent at it), then taking on another element will give you much better odds of successfully embedding your new routine into your life. It might take longer, but it's more likely that you'll sustain it. And slow and steady is the name of the game here.

Let's take a morning routine as an example. Your perfect routine might look like this:

1. waking up early
2. meditating
3. drinking a green smoothie
4. exercising
5. preparing a nourishing breakfast.

If you set off from a standing start and try to incorporate *all* of these elements for the first time, then you really do have your work cut out for you.

Instead, I suggest taking one habit, embedding it, then layering the other habits on top of that.

It would make sense for 'waking up early' to be the first cab off the rank, as that will buy you the time for everything else in your desired routine. So, for two weeks, set yourself the goal of waking up at your specified earlier time – and that's it. Use the extra time to have a longer shower, check your social media or get to the office a little earlier. Once this is embedded, pick up meditation.

For the two weeks after that, you not only get up earlier, you also meditate for ten minutes every day. Once you've got that nailed, you add the green smoothie. And so on …

With this approach, you are introducing a new layer to your routine every fortnight – and at the end of ten weeks you'll have the new routine built. And built to last.

Everyone's routine is going to be different

It's vitally important when building routines that we don't get too caught up in the routines of others.

Over the following pages, I'm going to share examples of the routines that successful people adopt. These are purely for inspiration and illustration purposes – I do not recommend that you try to copy someone else's routine in minute detail, due to the simple fact that they live a different life to you.

I'm going to share my morning and evening routine with you; however, I am not for a moment saying that they are the best routines – they're just the best for me and where I'm at in my life right now. In fact, as similar as myself and Wade's lifestyles are, our individual routines are completely different.

Remember that the routines that work for you are the ones that work for *you*. A routine that makes you feel like you're charging ahead in life could be utterly unhelpful for me, and vice versa.

Design the routine that works for you.

Test it.

Tweak it.

Perfect it.

Give yourself gold stars

In my business, The Remarkables Group, we embed our company values using personalised vision boards. Each member of the team has the four values of the business represented by four images that they chose themselves, which are then laminated and placed on their desk.

When someone displays one of those values, another person on the team can give them a gold star – and once they have twenty stars, they get Gold Class movie tickets for them and a friend. They give me gold stars, I give them gold stars, they give each other gold stars – it's a completely democratic process. It's an incredibly effective approach, and we get so excited when we attract a gold star. It gets quite competitive, too!

I have found that we never grow out of the thrill of getting our achievements chalked up somewhere visible where we ourselves and others can see tangible proof that we actually did it. It's like the five-year-old in their first year of school is still there, underneath all the layers of 'grown-up-ness'.

Think of rewards as petrol in the tank to keep you on your new path.

When you keep up the habit you're trying to ingrain, giving yourself a treat that will make you happy provides a mood-boosting pat on the back. You like the feeling of that pat on the back, and are even more motivated to earn the next one.

There are two types of rewards: extrinsic and intrinsic.

Extrinsic rewards are external to us – such as buying that new pair of shoes, having a massage, hiring that sports car for a day.

Intrinsic rewards are more about how we feel – so if we leave the office on time every day for a week, we feel proud of ourselves (and our partners probably love us that little bit more). Or if we hit our goal of going for three runs a week, we feel energised and accomplished.

Extrinsic rewards are better for short-term wins; however, intrinsic rewards lay the flagstones for us to sustain that new behaviour long term.

As I've already flagged, I am borderline obsessed with food so my rewards are generally eating related. For example, while writing this book, I've promised myself a visit to a local café for hot chocolate (dark chocolate with rosewater, to be precise) if I hit my daily word count target. For a more large-scale reward, it will be dinner at a fancy restaurant.

When I'm trying to embed a new habit in my life, I'll write it up on a scorecard on the fridge, which has ticks for every day of the week – as well as capturing a reward that I'll get to enjoy if I tick all the boxes.

I've used this method to get up earlier, reduce the amount of time I'm spending on social media, increase the number of exercise sessions I do, get a regular meditation practice going, read more, clean up my diet and even have more fun.

I cannot tell you how many times I've hauled my ass out of bed at 5.30 a.m. so I could tick the box, or contained myself to the sofa to do five minutes of meditation. It is a thing of enormous satisfaction to pause in front of the fridge before I go to bed at night and tick off that I completed that habit for the day.

For me, this is essentially a competition with myself, a competition that keeps me accountable. No one is going to prod me out of the bed in the morning. No one is going to take my phone off me because I already checked Instagram four times that evening. No one is going to ask me how my fledgling meditation practice is coming along.

Sadly, that's all my responsibility now – part and parcel of this thing we call adulting. Creating a super-simple little tool like this gives me something to aim for, and something to pat myself on the back for at the end of the week.

I've shared a free Weekly Habit Scorecard worksheet on my website, which is the exact structure I use. You can also purchase a pad of scorecards if you'd like to pop a pack on the fridge as you build new, sustainable habits into your daily life.

The GRO list

1. Identify three routines that you currently have running in your life – they can be constructive or not, intentional or accidental.
2. Ask yourself how well the routine (or lack of routine) in your life is serving you right now.
3. Identify one activity that you know sits at each level of competence.
4. Choose one thing that you do every day and articulate what the cue, action and reward are for it.
5. Consider creating your own personal tracking and reward system to help you build constructive habits into your life.

CHAPTER 6

Morning routine

Having explored the theory of routines and habits, let's get into the nitty-gritty of building some routines that will help you kick ass – every day.

As you know now, routines can be built into every part of your day, from your office morning tea break to your Saturday afternoon exercise schedule. There is one time of day that is of paramount importance to having a solid routine, though – and that's your morning.

Even if you have decided that routine isn't critical to you, I strongly suggest that you design even a light-on morning routine that will set you on your way for the day ahead.

> How we spend our mornings is the deciding factor for how the rest of the day will play out.

That time immediately after we wake up sets the tone for everything else that happens, until you jump back into bed again that night and the whole show starts over.

Steve Kay, a professor of molecular and computational biology at the University of Southern California, identifies a number of different reasons for the benefits of a morning routine:

1. Standardising the first 30–120 minutes with a routine lets you arrive at peak thinking time (i.e. mid-morning) in the best possible mindset.
2. A steady morning routine creates a rock in what can feel like a raging river. Regardless of how crazy your day could become, a morning routine gives you an anchor, a sense of normality to root yourself to.
3. Most importantly, a morning routine generates momentum.

The book *Daily Rituals: How Artists Work* examines the good work habits of more than 150 of the greatest writers, artists and scientists. It found that the majority of the people studied had not just a clear routine, but also shared a workday schedule of waking up early, working until midday, taking a break for a few hours then resuming work until dinner. Most seemed to use the evening hours for relaxation and socialising. This sounds like a pretty smart routine to me!

We have already discussed how every single person's routine will be unique to them – and each of us will also have a different threshold for how much routine we need to build into our lives in order to feel effective.

That's why this chapter isn't going to give you a fail-safe, one-size-fits-all, tried-and-tested morning routine that comes with a money-back guarantee.

Instead, it will outline the key objectives of a healthy morning routine, give you some resources to help you build a routine that works for you, and give you buckets of inspiration via insights into the morning routines of super-successful people.

Three things every morning routine should deliver

1. White space

In the world of graphic design, white space is the space that is not otherwise used for graphics, text, borders or margins. If there isn't enough white space on a page, the different elements appear to be competing against each other to be seen and the overall effect is cluttered and confusing. When white space is used well, there is balance to the page and our eyes can give adequate attention to each individual element without being overwhelmed.

Indeed, according to Wikipedia: 'White space should not be considered merely "blank" space — *it is an important element of design which enables the objects in it to exist at all*; the balance between positive (or non-white) and the use of negative spaces is key to aesthetic composition.'[1]

If the white space didn't exist, then all the elements on the page couldn't exist either.

When I speak to a group about getting organised, I often ask who checks their emails before they get out of bed in the morning. At least half of them will put up their hands – and usually another 10 per cent then follow when I remind everyone to answer honestly!

At the start of this book, I talked about the crazy demands

that simply existing in our modern world places upon us. We are expected to be always 'on' – and indeed we feel weird when we're *not* 'on'.

This starts the very second we wake up, and I truly believe that getting connected within a few minutes of waking up is a dangerous path to feeling disorganised. As Tristan Harris, Google's former design ethicist, says, looking at your phone immediately on waking can 'hijack' your morning routine.

This early morning connectedness can also negatively affect our mental health. It is no accident that, as the prevalence of smartphones and social media has increased in recent years, in parallel so have the instances of mental health issues like anxiety and depression.

The University of Chicago showed that social media is more addictive than cigarettes and harder to abstain from than a cocktail might be,[2] while a study from the Centre for Research on Media, Technology and Health at the University of Pittsburgh found that the more young adults use social media, the more likely they are to be depressed.[3]

Buddhist monk Thích Nhất Hanh notes that when we feel stressed, we're either ruminating on the past or worrying about the future. That's certainly true when you look at the laundry list of notifications on your phone – it makes you think about the things you need to do that day, rather than fully enjoying and being present in your morning.

When we wake up, roll over and pick up our phones to check our texts/emails/Facebook/Instagram/Snapchat/news headlines, we are instantaneously operating on the agenda of the outside world.

It's like the hamster in our brains has been safely ensconced in a world of REM, peace and quiet – and then we chuck a bucket of ice-cold water over it, jam a shot of espresso into its mouth, and kick it up the butt on the way to our day. I find it impossible to see how we could possibly be in the driving seat for the day ahead after a wake-up call like that!

Giving our little hamsters some white space first thing in the morning has multiple benefits:

1. It allows us to wake up *gently*.
2. It gives us time to process the thinking, dreaming and processing that we did overnight.
3. Most importantly, it pays ourselves first energetically – meaning we prioritise ourselves before we start to hand energy over to the rest of the world.

Pay yourself first

There's a concept in finance called 'paying yourself first'. It is beautiful in its simplicity.

Most people get paid and the first transactions they make are to businesses or individuals they need to pay – be it the bank for the mortgage, the landlord for rent or the electricity company for power. This sends out a powerful message to the universe – that they are more important than you.

Instead we should pay ourselves first.

This means putting x amount of money into a savings account, or putting a chunk of cash over to a transaction account to cover spending for the month ahead – before any other money leaves our bank account. This simple rearrangement of priorities states that *we* are more important than the countless third parties we give money to every day, and it's a subtle but powerful shift in energy.

By prioritising ourselves with a little white space in the morning, we make it clear that we are more important than the onslaught of information/requests/demands that come our way from the rest of the world every single day.

Having white space every morning is critically important to me. If I don't have it for whatever reason, I feel I've short-changed myself and I have a lingering sense of feeling slightly behind all day long – as well as being resentful of all the requests, questions and deadlines coming my way throughout the day.

There are many ways to create white space in your morning routine. For you, it might just be lying in bed for five minutes with no distractions. It might be meditating. It might be taking the time to make a cup of tea with no radio/TV blaring at you. It might be having a cuddle with your child. It might be journaling.

Almost without exception, the people I interviewed for this book had white space built into their mornings. For author and blogger Melissa Ambrosini, it's meditation. Entrepreneur Sabri Suby plays with his daughter and does some breathing exercises.

As I write this chapter, our little girl is three weeks old – meaning my usual morning routine has been put on hold while we adapt to having a whole new human to take care of. So, rather than my full morning routine (which I'll share with you shortly), I've made getting her sorted in the morning my white space. That means I don't take my phone off flight mode until she has had most of her breakfast, her nappy has been changed and she's dressed for the day.

> Building some white space into your morning routine means that you start the day on your terms, and not everyone else's terms.

The very act of creating that white space also enables the key elements of your life – be they family, career or health – to be seen to their fullest potential.

2. Focus

The second thing every morning routine should do is provide focus on what you want to achieve – not just on that day alone, but overall in your life.

Clear goals are something I believe all of us should have. Clear goals mean we have a destination in mind, and this enables us to work our way towards them by making key decisions on how we spend each day. If you would like some help on that front, I suggest you download the Setting Your Vision worksheets from my website – lorrainemurphy.com.au.

Taking just a few moments to check in on our goals in the morning is the ultimate way to keep us on track to actually achieving them. So many people set their goals at the start of January, then they sit on a shelf somewhere for the rest of the year.

Having our goals conveniently at hand means that we're reminding ourselves of them daily. Even if we're not actively thinking about them on a conscious level all day long, our brains are certainly bubbling away on a subconscious level to help us make them a reality.

Researcher Jennifer Milne, a PhD student at the University of Western Ontario, describes the unconscious mind as a 'semi-autonomous robot in our brain that plans and executes actions on our behalf with only the broadest of instructions from us'.[4]

The science backs up the power of writing down – and looking at – our goals. Dr Gail Matthews, a psychology professor at the Dominican University in California, recently studied the art and science of goal setting. She gathered 267 people comprising a diverse range of global locations, professions and sexes, and divided them into two groups. Group 1 wrote down their goals and dreams, while Group 2 didn't.

Dr Matthews found that those who wrote down their goals regularly saw those goals become a reality significantly more than those who didn't – in fact, the participants in Group 1 were *42 per cent more likely to achieve their goals* by writing them down and looking at them frequently.[5]

So why is this the case?

It comes down to neurology again.

When we think about our goals, we're using the right brain – the half that's imaginative, creative and big-thinking.

When we write down our goals, and look at them regularly, we engage the left hemisphere of the brain. This side is all about logic, action and focus.

So by thinking of our goals (right brain) and then writing them down (left brain), we achieve an unstoppable combination that sets us on the way to achievement of those ambitions.

I am a big fan of laminating my goals and putting them somewhere I'll see them every day. Right now, my annual goals live in a drawer next to the bed, but for many years I had them stuck up in the shower – so that looking at them didn't require extra time in the morning!

Entrepreneur and author of *The 10X Rule*, Grant Cardone, writes each of his goals out longhand as soon as he wakes up every day. You might spend a few minutes looking at your vision board for how you see your dream life. Or you might have a set of affirmations that you say out loud every morning.

I love the example of Jim Carrey. In the early 1990s, Carrey was an unknown actor struggling to get by. To stay motivated, he decided to write himself a cheque for $10 million for 'acting services rendered', dated it 1994 and carried it in his wallet for daily inspiration. When 1994 rolled around, he found out his fee for starring in *Dumb and Dumber* would be precisely $10 million.

In an interview with MTV in 2009, singer Katy Perry shared that she made a vision board in school when she was nine. She cut out a photo of Latina pop singer Selena holding a Grammy award. Fifteen years later, and Perry was holding her own golden statuette after winning her first Grammy.

Focusing on the immediate day ahead is also key. This might mean you consult your to-do list for the day, have a chat with your partner about who's doing what with the kids or write a time plan for how you're going to spend the day.

Injecting some focus into your morning routine will look different for everyone, so find what works for you and stick to that.

3. Energy

If we want our morning routine to set the tone for the entire day ahead, does it make sense to spend it pursuing energy-zapping activities such as checking smartphones and keeping up with social media? Of course not!

Nor should you force yourself to drag your sorry ass around a bootcamp every morning while hating every second if it only depletes your energy – however, a twenty-minute walk around the block could give you the perfect power-up for the day ahead.

The point is to include something in your morning routine that *builds* your energy. That energy might not necessarily come from physical activity, either.

I prefer to exercise later in the day and I love cooking, so my energy fuel in the morning comes from preparing a delicious breakfast for myself. That gives me not only an energetic boost, but a nutritional one, too. Entrepreneur Peter Moriarty has 'morning music' and burns specific aromatic oils and incense to activate his energy for the day ahead.

It's smart to find at least one activity in the morning that will give you an energy boost. See it as giving you the momentum energetically for the day ahead.

The Miracle Morning

I would describe myself as having had a loose morning routine until early last year, when I read a book that quite honestly changed my life. I really think you should read it too.

Hal Elrod had what you might call the classic 'down and out' story – his health was poor, his relationships were defunct, his career was non-existent and his finances were in such a poor state that he was living on friends' sofas.

He was in a perennial state of feeling he should be doing more with his life – more exercise, more reading, more goal-setting ... He was in a downward spiral of negativity: the more time he spent in this crappy state, the less inclined he was to get himself out of it.

One day, he had something of an epiphany. What if he got up the next morning and actually did the empowering exercises he'd been saying he'd do more of – all together? He went to sleep that night excited for the morning to roll around: in his own words, it felt like Christmas!

The next morning, he ran, he read, he meditated, he recited some affirmations.

And then he did again the next morning, and the morning after that. The effect was completely transformational. He reinvigorated his career, lost 20 kilograms and overall was the happiest he'd ever been.

The result of this little experiment was his book *The Miracle Morning*, which has gone on to transform many other lives.[6]

There is a lot of very, very good stuff on morning routines in the book; however, one element that I will pull out for your benefit now is the concept of LifeSAVERS, which is the core structure to any Miracle Morning.

The LifeSAVERS are:

S – Silence

A – Affirmations

V – Visualisation

E – Exercise

R – Reading

S – Scribing

What Hal recommends is that we design our own Miracle Morning that incorporates each of these individual elements:

- **Silence** is the 'white space' that we covered earlier in this chapter. You will have your own interpretation of what works best for you.
- **Affirmations** are sayings or quotes that we say aloud to ourselves every morning, as a way of keeping us in tune with the people we want to be or the goals we want to achieve.
- **Visualisation** is actively picturing ourselves attaining a goal, or having something that we fervently wish to have. Many athletes make excellent use of the power of visualisation by mentally rehearsing their victory in lucid detail before the race, game or match begins.
- **Exercise** speaks for itself – whatever physical activity you enjoy and is accessible for you to spend some time doing every day.
- **Reading** is not your Instagram feed – sorry. It's motivational, inspirational or educational texts. It might be a magazine article, a book you've been meaning to read forever or an online article you tagged to come back to later on.
- **Scribing** is some kind of morning writing. I love to journal, so for me scribing is filling a page in my journal every morning.

There's another tool you might like to try, called Morning Pages; it was designed by author Julia Cameron, and involves writing three pages of text longhand every morning. She describes the technique as 'spiritual windshield wipers'.

There's no structure to it: you just flow with whatever pops into your brain and onto the paper it goes. I haven't practised it myself, but several people have told me that they have gained enormous clarity and peace from it.

Author of *The 4-Hour Workweek*, Tim Ferris, is one high-profile fan of Morning Pages. The benefit for him? In his own words: 'I'm just caging my monkey mind on paper so I can get on with my fucking day.'

This all sounds like a terrible lot to do just for one morning, doesn't it? Never mind trying to find the time to do it every single morning!

The true beauty of the Miracle Morning, in my opinion, is that it doesn't need to take hours of time. In fact, Hal can complete all six LifeSAVERS *in just sixty minutes.*

Exercise doesn't need to involve a full ninety-minute yoga class; it can instead be ten minutes of YouTube yoga stretches on the bedroom floor or fifteen minutes jogging around the block with the dog.

Ditto for reading – Hal doesn't suggest we read two hours of a weighty tome every morning, but instead spend just 5–10 minutes investing our brains in some quality material.

When I started practising Miracle Mornings, I had been meaning to read Tony Robbins' *Unlimited Power* for years previously, but the denseness of the book put me off getting properly started. By spending ten minutes each morning gradually chipping away at it, I completed the book in six weeks.

The piecemeal approach actually worked in my favour, as over the day I had time to process the (sometimes complex) ideas Tony shared before moving on to the next part the following morning.

Hal even suggests a six-minute Miracle Morning for those of us who are especially time-pressed, or on those mornings when an hour simply can't be found – for example, when you have an early meeting at work or the kids decide to invade your bedroom extra early. This involves spending just one minute on each of the LifeSAVERS – you should try it, it's fun!

Finding the time for a morning routine

You'll probably need to wake up earlier. It's that simple.

I have noticed a strong trend among successful people of also being early risers. In fact, not one of the people I interviewed as I wrote this book rises later than 7 a.m.

Author Kelly Exeter swears by her morning routine and she also likes to have a couple of hours to write before her husband and two kids wake up. In order to do this, she needs to wake up at 4.15 a.m. Even on weekends.

She spends this time writing, exercising and browsing through social media. Her two daily non-negotiables (going back to our chat about standards in Chapter 4) are writing and exercising, so ticking those two boxes before the rest of the household rises sets her up for the day ahead.

This approach is shared by other success stories: Apple CEO Tim Cook also wakes at 4 a.m. However, it's important to accept that 4 a.m. wake-up calls may not work for you – I know they don't work for me, having tried for weeks to get into the swing of waking up at 5 a.m. (By the way, The 5 a.m. Club actually exists – as a book, and an app – if you want to try it.)

Up until a few years ago, I woke up at around 7.30 a.m as standard. I would be on the clock most mornings to get to the office by 9 a.m. and if I'm honest it was more like 9.05 or 9.10 when I arrived. If I had to wake up earlier to catch a flight – for example, by 6 a.m. – I would feel it *all day long.* My body just wasn't used to it.

I realised that I needed to create more time in my mornings as I got fed up with the rushing. Moving to Australia also helped – Aussies like to get up early!

I set myself a micro goal of setting my alarm fifteen minutes earlier. Once that became a habit, I set it another fifteen minutes earlier, and so on. Over the course of a few short months, I was in the habit of waking up at 6 a.m. – and very often I didn't even need my alarm to wake me anymore!

This meant I could do a Pilates class, go for a walk or simply have a bit more time to get ready in the morning. Then as I became aware of the power of a positive morning routine, I found I had already created the window of time to complete one as I was in the habit of getting up earlier.

This comes back to knowing what is the bare minimum time that you need as you start to build a morning routine. You might start off with ten minutes of white space and go from there, which means setting the alarm ten minutes earlier. Or joining The 5 a.m. Club might work for you.

Each of us will have an optimum wake-up time that means we rise feeling rested, yet still allows us to complete the morning routine we desire. For me, waking up between 5.30 and 6 a.m. is perfect.

Another challenge many of you may have is that little chestnut of small people who demand much of the early hours of your day – an adventure I'm finding myself on for the first time right now!

A few thoughts for you if you're in this position:

1. Would it be possible for you to time your wake-up thirty minutes before the kids' eyes pop open?
2. Could you practise your morning routine a little later in the day, perhaps when they're napping?
3. Would it work better for you to practise the elements of the Miracle Morning in the evening when the little ones are in bed?
4. Could you commit to a ten-minute morning routine three days a week?

I cannot overstate the fact that a morning routine needs to work for *you* and the lifestyle that *you* have right now.

My morning routine

Purely for illustration purposes, I'll share with you how my morning routine generally runs:

5.30 a.m.	Alarm goes off (I've weaned myself off the snooze button).
5.35 a.m.	Get out of bed, use bathroom.
5.40 a.m.	Go the kitchen and put the kettle on, tidy away dishes on draining board from night before, remove from the fridge the lemon drinks prepared the night before and add hot water.
5.50 a.m.	Go back to bed and take my Miracle Morning bits and pieces out of the drawer in my bedside table.
5.50 a.m.	Set my phone timer for twenty minutes and meditate.

6.10 a.m.	Do a reading using two sets of oracle cards.
6.15 a.m.	Read my affirmations aloud (on one page, laminated).
6.17 a.m.	Read through my goals (on one page, also laminated).
6.20 a.m.	Write in my journal – fill a page.
6.30 a.m.	Read part of a book.
6.40 a.m.	Take my phone off airplane mode, check text messages and social media (I never check my emails until later in the morning).
7.00 a.m.	Get up – do hair and make-up, get dressed.
7.15 a.m.	Make the bed.
7.20 a.m.	Cook and eat breakfast.
7.50 a.m.	Pack bag for day – gym gear, lunch, anything else I'll need.
8.00 a.m.	Leave the house.

Your morning routine can be as sedate and structured or wild and wacky as you want it to be.

Benjamin Franklin described his as, 'I rise early almost every morning, and sit in my chamber without any clothes whatever, half an hour or an hour, according to the season, either reading or writing.'

Victor Hugo, author of *Les Misérables*, was awakened by the daily gunshot from the fort near his home, had a cup of freshly brewed coffee while reading a letter from his mistress, Juliette Drouet, and then drank two raw eggs.

The GRO list

1. Think about what your standard morning routine looks like – write it down.
2. Consider the idea of white space in your morning – do you have a lot or none at all?
3. Read *The Miracle Morning*.
4. Having read this chapter, design what the perfect morning routine *for you* would look like.
5. Ask yourself honestly if you could create more time in your morning by getting up earlier.
6. If you want to create an earlier rising habit, use the Weekly Habit Scorecard from my website – lorrainemurphy.com.au – and reward yourself accordingly.
7. If a chunk of time simply isn't available to you every morning, identify opportunities to access that time at other points in the day.
8. Remember to layer up habits gradually until you arrive at your perfect morning routine – don't put yourself under too much pressure if this is all new to you!

CHAPTER 7

Evening routine

The second time of day that it helps enormously to have a well-embedded routine is the evening.

Generally my evening routine is more fluid than my morning routine, due to the fact that meetings, events and social catch-ups happen so I'm not in a position to dictate timings as much I can in the mornings. I might get home at 6.30 p.m. via a yoga class, or 11 p.m. because I went to an awards night.

Even if I'm getting to bed at midnight (a *lot* later than my usual bedtime!), there are a few basic elements that I will complete before I crash out.

Just like the morning routines we've already discussed, your evening routine needs to be specially tailored for you. There are, however, a few objectives that a successful evening routine should achieve, regardless of how you approach it personally.

Three things every evening routine should deliver

1. Closure

No, I don't mean sending your ex from five years ago an emo email *finally* getting those last niggles about their behaviour off your chest!

> A key element in our evening routine is effectively 'closing down' the day we just had, essentially drawing a line under it so that we can approach the next day with a fresh perspective.

It can be very energy draining to be thinking and rethinking the events of the day, and especially any loose ends that we didn't get to tie up.

If we can wrap up the day that just occurred with a neat bow around it, we can capture any learnings, review our progress and set ourselves up for success the following day.

One super-easy and effective way for me to achieve this 'closing down' is to review my to-do list at the end of the day. I tick off the items I got done, and circle those that need to be done the following day.

If there are actions that need to be carried over (and there always are), then I pause for a second to see whether it would make more sense to delegate that task for someone else to do the next day.

I then write my to-do list for the following day, which helps for a few reasons:

1. It effectively draws a line under the day that has just occurred and any loose ends are captured on a list.
2. It eliminates the 'must do that tomorrow' mental circles that are so pointless and tiring.
3. It delivers a speedier start the following morning as the first ten minutes of the day don't need to be spent writing a to-do list.

A gratitude practice is another great way to close down the day. This can be as sophisticated or as simple as you like. Personally, I go for the simple route and mentally list five things I'm grateful for that day before I go to sleep.

I know several people who maintain gratitude journals – in book or online format. Journaling at night might be an excellent way for you to debrief on your day, and prepare you for the next day.

> Find one way of closing down at the end of each day, then practise it until it's a habit and is embedded into your evening routine.

2. Preparedness for the next day

Probably the most important thing for me about my evening routine is that, once it's successfully completed, I'm feeling fully prepared for the next day.

This can often feel like an utter pain in the ass, especially when I've gotten home later than usual or I'm wiped after a day of six meetings. The benefits the next morning, however, make the extra twenty minutes the night before so, so worth it.

You might notice from my morning routine in the previous chapter that there is little to no preparation involved – instead I spend the time doing my Miracle Morning, making myself look human and enjoying a delicious breakfast. No lunches are made, no gym gear is scrabbled together and no clothes are picked out – all of that happens the night before.

You'll know already from Chapter 4 that food is one of the areas to which I apply high standards – and as such, it requires significant time and energy to maintain those standards. The last thing I want to be doing in the morning is cobbling together a day of food rations, as it would consume far too much time. It's also not as enjoyable a task when there's a time limit on it.

As activities vary more in my evenings, I don't have set timings when certain things get done – instead it's more of a checklist approach. Between the time I arrive in the door and switch off the bedside light, I aim to complete the following tasks:

Unpack – time taken: 10 minutes
- Unpack the inevitable extra bag I'll have had with me during the day – which can include any combination of lunch containers, jars, heels, laptop, laptop charger, phone charger, books, meeting notes, mail.
- Everything is allocated to its proper home – the dishwasher for food containers, my home office for my laptop, wardrobe for clothes, and so on.

Food – time taken: 1 hour 15 minutes (if I'm doing this myself, less if Wade is with me)
- Cook dinner, or heat leftovers from the night before.
- Wash as I cook so that clean-up is minimal.

- Enjoy dinner at the dining table with no distractions.
- Tidy away dishes.
- Prepare lunch for the following day.
- Prepare a lemon drink for the following morning – that means, juice a lemon and split it between two mugs, half fill with water, then store in the fridge. The following morning we just need to boil the kettle and fill the mugs.
- Prepare green smoothies for the following day.
- Prepare an afternoon snack.
- Leave the kitchen clean and clear for the following morning.

Clothes – time taken: 10 minutes
- Dump any dirty clothes in the laundry basket.
- Check my meetings for the next day to decide how casual/smart I need to be.
- Check the weather for the next day.
- Pull out an outfit, right down to the matching underwear and shoes.
- If I'm exercising the next day, pull out my gym gear and put it into my bag.

Written down like this, it seems like a huge amount of work! The beauty of this routine, though, is that it's fully automatic for me.

I used to spend fifteen minutes every morning frantically trying to decide what to wear for the day ahead, which didn't help my stress levels trying to get out the door. I find my decision-making when it comes to clothes is a lot quicker in the evening than the morning – it seems to take twice as long at the start of the day. Knowing exactly what clothes I'm going to step into when I get up makes my morning just that bit easier, and – as a direct result – my entire day that bit easier, too.

Co-founder of Show + Tell, Stacey Morlang Sullivan, articulates this 'I got this' feeling perfectly: 'I'm very careful about preparing everything the night before each day. If I don't do that, I feel very out of control.'

There are definitely evenings when the Can't Be Fucked Index is at an all-time high, and on the following days I may need to get a takeaway lunch. It is amazing, though, how much more quickly I can tick through these things when I'm tired and my comfortable bed is an enticing incentive to get it done!

I am going to repeat here that everyone's evening routine will be as unique to them as their morning routine is. You know by now what areas are of priority in your life, and what standards you're aiming to achieve – so deciding how to weight your evening routine time should be relatively simple.

As you can tell from my standard routine, it doesn't accommodate having a family or regular evening commitments – so it may not work for someone who does have either of those things that they need to factor into their lifestyles. (I wrote the draft of this chapter before our baby's arrival. Needless to say, things have changed a little since then!)

3. Preparation for great sleep

We talked briefly about the importance of sleep in Chapter 3, and the fact that there are a *lot* of similarities between the mental capacity of a drunk person and that of a tired person.

You may hold your liquor (as our American friends say) a lot better than me; however, I know that I feel significantly more organised *before* four vodka sodas than afterwards!

> Sleep really is a core bedrock to the overall success of our lives.

Author and founder of HuffPost, Arianna Huffington, wrote at length about the importance of getting a good night's rest in her book *Thrive*. The response to her shout-out for us to get more zzz's was so powerful that her next book, *The Sleep Revolution*, focused specifically on the benefits of sleep – and how to get more of it.

A portion of my evening routine is always devoted to setting myself up for a great night's sleep – which means falling asleep easily, staying asleep and waking up rested the next morning.

Again, instead of specific times, this takes a checklist structure:

1. Know that (as much as possible) everything is prepared for the next day of activities – so food is ready to go, clothes are pulled out and any documents/items I need to take with me the next day are already packed in my bag.
2. Lights in the bedroom are low.
3. The phone is on flight mode from when I go into the bedroom.
4. Close the windows and drop the blinds.
5. Put a few drops of a sleep-inducing essential oil blend into the oil diffuser and switch it on. This

is something I discovered during some pregnancy-related insomnia and it has made my sleep all the better. I wake sometimes during the night – worrying, planning and thinking – like I imagine most of us do at times. So I get up and switch the diffuser on again, and I almost always fall straight back asleep.

6. Pull the fan out of the wardrobe and switch it on for white noise.

7. Get into bed.

8. Apply lavender essential oil to my temples.

9. Read for about half an hour. My reading material at night is something easy and reassuring. I don't read business books or thrillers around bedtime. Instead, it will be 'easy' non-fiction, historical books or my favourite children's books. (I'm just coming out of a lengthy *Little House on the Prairie* phase!)

10. Turn out the light and list in my head the five things for which I'm most grateful that happened during the day. This also provides another way of 'closing down' the day I've just had.

11. Generally fall asleep within five minutes.

You can see from our earlier discussion of what a routine is (a chain of habits linked together) that here I essentially have eleven habits that all build to make up my evening routine.

Think back to Charles Duhigg's three elements of a habit – the cue, the action and the reward – and they apply quite neatly to sleep. We create cues (be it scents, lighting or performing certain activities), that lead to an action (falling and staying asleep), resulting in a reward (waking up refreshed the following morning).

Each of these small actions I complete every night acts as a mini cue for the others – with each following the previous one fluidly. The compound effect of all of them together is, generally speaking, a solid night's sleep.

Back to our friend Ben Franklin ... before going to bed each night at midnight, he would ask himself, 'What good have I done today?'

Bill Gates reads for an hour before bed, regardless of what time he arrives home. And he's in good company with that habit. Arianna Huffington only reads 'real books' before bed. She recommends banning iPads, Kindles, laptops and any other electronics from the bedroom to unwind.

Founder of The Entourage, Jack Delosa, stops working at 8 p.m. to ensure he has a couple of hours to switch off and ground himself, as he has found this crucial to getting a good night's sleep. Entrepreneur Sabri Suby has a self-imposed phone ban from 6 p.m., while another entrepreneurial friend of mine, Peter Moriarty, kicks off the evening with music and incense or scented oils.

The GRO list

1. Consider your evening routine right now (if you have one) and ask yourself whether you are currently ticking off the three objectives of an evening routine (closure, preparedness for the next day, and sleep preparation).

2. If one particular area – or all three – is lacking, identify *just one thing* you could do in that area to help you start to lock down an effective evening routine that works for you personally.
3. Start to track your sleep using an app or wearable technology, and observe how the steps you take as part of your evening routine are helping you to get more rest.
4. Don't forget the importance of layering small habits until they build the routine you want – remember that slow, steady and sustainable trumps radical overnight life overhauls any day!

CHAPTER 8

Organising your week

Designing your Perfect Week

I am a big fan of the Perfect Day exercise – which is a blank day broken down into thirty-minute chunks of time. The idea is that you design what a perfect day looks like for you, and then you endeavour to make that a reality (as much as you can) every day. I created a worksheet to help readers do this – you can download it for free from the store on my website: lorrainemurphy.com.au.

As a starting point, while you get your remarkably organised training wheels on, it would be a useful exercise for you to map out what your *Perfect Week* also looks like. To help you do this, I've created a Perfect Week worksheet – also available on my website.

The idea of creating your Perfect Week is to help you design how you would spend your week if all the stars aligned and you got to devote your time to the activities, people and commitments that are most important in how you want to live your life.

For some of us, this will mean factoring in six work-outs a week; for others, it will be ensuring there's an afternoon of Netflix binge-watching. Some of us will want a full hour to meditate every morning, while some of us will block out a solid four hours for a long boozy lunch with friends on a Saturday afternoon.

This is *your* time to dream, create and manifest, so make the perfect week one that will get you excited and motivated – and, most importantly, one that will make you happy.

The chance of us executing our perfect week every single week is unlikely with the curve balls and demands that life often sends our way; however, the first step in making a dream a reality is to articulate it clearly.

I would not be the slightest bit surprised if you plan your perfect week today, and in a couple of months' time your real-life week is looking freakishly like the one you planned. That's the crazy thing about sending a clear signal to the Universe ... Things tend to happen *exactly* like we requested them to happen.

The weekly planning session

When I ask people what is one of the biggest take-outs from *Remarkability* that has helped them to get more organised, a frequent response is 'the idea to plan planning time'.

> Setting aside a period of time that is specially designated to map out your week ahead is by far one of the quickest ways to get back on top of the crazy-busyness that is most of our lives.

Research has shown that for every one minute you spend planning, you get ten minutes back in execution. So, for example, if you spend ten minutes planning a task, you'll save one hour and forty minutes in performing that task.[1] This is why planning your week is so critical, as by investing some time upfront considering everything you need to do, you shave hours – literally – off the time taken to actually do everything.

How cool is that?!

Imagine if we took the time to plan every single task we undertake – we'd get shit done in a tenth of the time! If you managed to gain just an extra thirty minutes per day by managing your time more effectively, you could credit a whole twenty-two days back into your year overall. Imagine what you could do with an extra three weeks a year ... The mind boggles.

It also makes us better at our jobs. The Energy Project's president and CEO, Tony Schwartz, explains in a story published by Business Insider that when his company surveyed 20,500 workers in cooperation with Harvard Business School, respondents who said they were able to plan and then focus on one task at a time reported being 50 per cent more engaged with their jobs than those who were not able to do this.[2]

I save in a big way on the time taken to do things during the week by taking the time to map out my week in advance.

A second reason why I plan my week in advance is that it saves my sanity. I would lose my mind taking the week on a day-by-day basis, not being across what's happening until I'm in that twenty-four-hour period. I know for a fact that until I started planning my week at the beginning of each week, I did less exercise, didn't eat as well, had too many meetings on a particular day and didn't succeed in ticking off my key to-do list items.

Third, it prevents me from heading into Overwhelm Territory. I'm sure you've been to this particularly unpleasant place yourself at times – where the work, commitments and to-do list are stacking up and you're starting to lose sleep about how the fuck you'll get it all done.

> Having a clear visual of the next seven days is a fail-safe way to get a 'helicopter view' of what's coming up, and provides time to shift things around if life is getting too hectic.

Finally, planning the week in advance makes me less flakey. Before I started doing this, I would accept meeting invites and social catch-ups as and when they dropped in, or whenever I was in touch with a friend. Hey presto, Wednesday evening rolls around and that dinner date I had planned is looking extremely unappealing as I've had six meetings that day and just want to sit on the sofa solo and rock my tender introverted self quietly. It seems I'm not alone in this. A recent *New York Times* article described this current period we live in as 'the golden age of bailing', mainly as technology makes it so easy for us to change plans at the last minute.

When I forecast my plans for seven days, I can see that with a highly social/busy Wednesday, I should probably book in some chill time and move dinner to Thursday. Figuring this out the Saturday prior, rather than at 3 p.m. on Wednesday, means that I can move commitments gracefully and minimise disruptions to other people.

I'm not the only one who advocates planning your week in advance. Of all the successful people I spoke to while gleaning organisational insights for this book, just one said that they didn't plan their week in advance.

Okay, have I got you convinced on this yet? Let's look at planning your week.

Weekly planning time

For me, this time usually lands on a Saturday and it's 30–45 minutes that I take to check in on what's already happening for the week ahead, and schedule in the various different commitments that help me take care of the areas of my life – from my relationship with Wade to my fitness.

How you approach this will be completely unique to you – each of you will develop your own blend of what needs to be booked in for the week ahead and the different tools you engage to do that.

You will definitely need a calendar of some sort. At this point in technology, I would assume that your calendar is likely to be on a device, although I do know people who are valiantly clinging on to their paper diaries – which is admirable, if rather quaint. However, maybe they have a point, as Richard Branson and Warren Buffet still use paper planners.

I use Google Calendar as it syncs neatly with my different devices, our business set-up is via Google and – most importantly for me – it enables me to colour code my diary prettily.

How to plan your week

Step 1: Review everything that's already in your calendar and ask yourself three questions:

1. Do I need to do this?

I've found that quite often I'll book in something weeks in advance – for example, a meeting. By the time the meeting rolls around, it's not actually required anymore and I might be able to deal with it via a phone call or email, or delegate attending the meeting to one of my team – quite often buying myself back the hour I had committed to the meeting, plus the travel time there and back.

2. Do I want to do this?

We say yes to an awful lot of commitments that, actually, we don't really want to keep. It might be coffee with a friend whose company doesn't excite us hugely, or a seminar that we feel we *should* attend as we haven't done anything to feed our brains for a while. I personally have been making a conscious effort to only commit to things I really *want* to do because, well, life is too short to spend hours per week doing shit I don't enjoy.

3. Does this need to be done this week?

When my week is looking especially full, I will get my Subtraction Hat on and move anything non-urgent by a week or two to inject some breathing space into the following seven days.

A significant percentage of the meetings I have from week to week are not time-sensitive – for example, having a coffee with someone who wants to 'pick my brains' on something (I hate that phrase, but I digress ...), or a team strategy session for a project that isn't launching for months yet.

If your week coming up is already looking out of control, I suggest you get your own Subtraction Hat on and cancel/ move a few non-urgent commitments out of the next seven days.

Step 2: Reschedule anything that needs to be moved

The key to smoothly rearranging our weeks is to give others plenty of notice if we need to move a commitment with them. It's vital that we're respectful of other people's time, and moving a meeting scheduled for Thursday on the Monday beforehand is a hell of a lot more polite than moving it on Thursday morning.

If you plan out the week ahead and know you'll need to move something, email/text/call as part of your weekly planning session. This gives other people the opportunity to book something else into that time – plus it's one less thing for your to-do list on Monday morning!

Step 3: Book in your non-negotiables

Non-negotiables are the tasks, meetings or commitments that absolutely *must* happen in your week. You'll likely find that your non-negotiables align with the areas of your life where you have high standards (from Chapter 4). The idea behind scheduling non-negotiables is that if they're in the diary, they need to happen.

Remember the concept of 'paying yourself first' that we discussed in Chapter 6? I like to think that planning in my non-negotiables at the start of the week is paying myself first with my valuable time. Remembering that time is the only resource we can never get back, I want – as much as is humanly possible – to invest my time in the areas of my life that I hold most precious.

What these non-negotiables are will vary from person to person; however, to give you an idea, mine are:

- weekly team meetings (management meeting with my business partner, catch-up with my assistant and other team check-ins)
- exercise classes
- quality time with Wade and Lexi.

I used to loosely commit to a yoga class after work, and bring my gear to the office with me. But if my day became hectic, or I just couldn't be arsed getting a sweat up, I'd skip the yoga and go straight on home.

When I started the business, having regular exercise became more of an urgent requirement – a) for the mental clarity that exercise gave me, and b) as I needed to stay as healthy as I could, given that there was no one else to run the business if I got sick. And so I started to diarise the exercise I wanted to do – hey presto, I immediately got fitter.

To me, a yoga or pilates class in my diary is a meeting with myself. I tell myself that I wouldn't cancel a meeting with a client or one of my team ten minutes before I was due to be there, so why would I do that to myself? This has gotten my tired/unmotivated/lazy ass into the yoga studio countless times!

Entrepreneur Sabri Suby says that his non-negotiable is sleep. For co-founder of SWIISH Maha Koraiem, it's a half-day at the weekend where she has nowhere to be and nothing to do. For blogger Alexx Stuart, it's walks.

You'll know yourself what your non-negotiables are – time with your kids, time to pray, a lie-in on a Sunday. Whatever they are, book them in at the beginning of the week and you immediately boost your chances of actually making them a reality.

Step 4: Plan your recreational time

I picked this tip up years ago when I first read Siimon Reynold's book *When They Zig, You Zag*. The book is made up of snippets of advice to avoid living an average life, and therefore getting average results.

Siimon states the importance of planning his weekend, just like he would the time he spends working in his business. So many of us don't plan out our weekend days, and I totally get why – we are so committed Monday to Friday that a little flow and breathing space feels in order for our precious downtime. The problem is that if I don't plan in all the things I'd like to do, I spend much of the weekend trying to decide what to do next and Sunday night rolls around all too quickly – at which point I'm feeling like I didn't get 'value' from the weekend.

On a Friday, I will generally do a time plan for the weekend approaching – when I map in when I'll do yoga, when I'll sleep in, when I'll get that walk out in nature. This helps me get the most out of my weekend, but also helps me achieve a state of enjoyment. I'm doing things with purpose, and the weekend has a wonderful flow to it as a result.

Step 5: Pre-book recurring appointments

This was a small off-the-cuff tip that I shared in Remarkability, which seems to have had an extraordinary impact. In it, I explained that I pre-book regular appointments for the year ahead – for example, a hair appointment every two months. This means that I'm guaranteed the timeslot I want and I do away with that irritating 'have to book my hair appointment' mental note. If you have an appointment you keep on an ongoing basis – be it physio, eyelash extensions or a monthly tennis date – try booking them in for the rest of the year now and see how much more organised you feel!

Step 6: Check off your week against your life priorities

Remember the Organisational Wheel from Chapter 4? You may find it useful to check off your week against your key life areas as you find your stride with your weekly planning session.

Compare the areas you ranked as having a high priority against how you're committing your time for the next seven days. Is the time you're allocating to each area in line with how high a priority it is?

You won't get the balance right every week; however, it may be a red flag if you have placed relationships with family and friends as a top priority, yet you're not getting any time with them over the next week. If this becomes a consistent theme, then it would be a good idea to revisit how you're planning your weeks.

Step 7: Allow buffer time

Urgent things will *always* drop into our calendars, which is why it makes me very nervous when my week ahead is already booked out – and it's only Saturday.

Having every hour accounted for in advance is a recipe for disaster – for me anyway. It means that when a fire needs to be fought in the business, or I need to free up time to see a key client so we can sign off on a new project, the time is simply not available.

This means moving something else at the last minute, sending myself into a tailspin trying to multitask between meetings, or having to hold off until the following week – and therefore delaying progress or letting whatever the fire was rage on unabated until I have the time and headspace to deal with it.

Just like the morning routine, it's key to factor in some white space when we're planning our weeks. Best-case scenario, we don't need it and we have an extra few hours of productivity up our sleeves. Worst-case scenario, the white space gets eaten up with something urgent – if this happens, it's not consuming time that was scheduled elsewhere.

I make it my mission to ensure that there is at least two hours of white space available every day – any less and I know the upcoming week will be more stressful than it needs to be.

Step 8: Colour code your week

As I mentioned earlier, I love the ability that Google Calendar provides me with to allocate a colour for each entry in my calendar. I've developed a little colour-coded system, so that at a glance I can tell where my time is being spent for the week ahead.

My code goes like this:

- Blue – business time
- Turquoise – health time (exercise classes, osteopath appointments)
- Pink – time with Wade (quality time, like a date night or evening hang-out on the sofa)
- Purple – time with friends or family
- Gold – spiritual/self-care time (e.g. my monthly kinesiology session, massages)
- Orange – life admin/grooming (our recent house move and associated tasks, hair appointments, etc.)

You might find colour coding helpful for you, too – if nothing else, it's more interesting to look at!

Some handy ideas for planning your week

No-meeting days

I have a policy of having no meetings at all on a Monday and no external meetings on a Friday.

Meetings – in fact, any diary commitment – are not just about the thirty minutes or hour they're scheduled for.

There's the travel time to and from the meeting, the prep required to do it (be that researching the person we're meeting on LinkedIn, or dragging a hairbrush through our hair), and the mental energy required to ensure we're on time for the meeting, fully prepared and have successfully worked out the logistics to attend it.

Even though travel time doesn't apply to phone calls, Skype meetings or Google hang-outs, all the rest applies to them just as much.

I maximise my productivity by solely devoting Mondays to getting shit done, with nowhere to be and no make-up required.

Fridays are for tying up loose ends from the week and catching up with the team about our weeks – plus getting a handle on the following week with them.

Of course, this means that Tuesday, Wednesday and Thursday are rather full – and generally I'm zipping about the city seeing clients, industry contacts and various other people.

I find that when I'm in the meeting zone, it's easier to stay in that zone and 'bookending' the week with days to get all the non-meeting tasks done works perfectly for me.

Consider designating one day a week – or even one morning a week – as a meeting- or commitment-free zone, and use this time to crack through your to-do list.

Maker versus Manager

I met an industry friend, Matt Kendall, a few months ago, who explained the concept of the Maker's schedule versus the Manager's schedule. The idea is that we have two distinct mindsets when it comes to work:

1. Maker – we're in the zone of working, creating, pumping product
2. Manager – we're out in meetings, building relationships, checking progress, pressing the flesh.

Paul Graham, a tech investor, created the model and explains that Makers are individuals with a specific skillset who need long, uninterrupted stretches of time in order to complete their tasks.

On the other hand, Managers spend their time in meetings (preparing for them, attending them, following up after them) as their role is to coordinate teams and deliver projects.

Many of us will have a hybrid of both schedules – including me. For example, when I need to be on the Maker's schedule, it will be for doing things like writing this book, mapping out a new strategy for the business or building a new client presentation from scratch. To do all of those things, I need to be 100 per cent in the zone – and not have to speak to other humans.

However, I also need to spend a significant chunk of my week on the Manager's schedule (probably more than the Maker's) – so this means having update meetings with the team, catch-ups with clients and the usual handful of networking coffee chats.

For example, my Wednesday might look like this:

8.00 a.m.	Breakfast meeting (Manager)
9.30 a.m.	Into the office to write a strategy (Maker)
11.00 a.m.	Team meeting to check in on a project (Manager)
12.00 p.m.	Random stuff – emails, lunch, mini catch-ups with team (Manager)
2.30 p.m.	Monthly finance update with our financial controller (Manager)
4.00 p.m.	Back on the strategy (Maker)

Days like this used to drive me nuts – and it was only when I got my head around the Maker vs Manager concept that I understood why those days feel stressful. It's because I'm trying to switch back and forth between each mode, when in fact I should contain each mode to specific days.

As Paul Graham explains, one meeting when you're trying to be on the Maker's schedule can blow out an entire day – even if it's in the afternoon, you're probably less likely to start something ambitious in the morning as you know you'll probably get pulled away from it.

A much better way to approach this would be to work on the strategy on my No Meeting Monday, when I know I'll have juicy stretches of uninterrupted time. Then on Tuesday, I book in meetings with gusto – knowing that a) I have the strategy done, and b) I can stay in the flow state of my meetings.

It's important to note here that virtual channels (and not just calls or face-to-face meetings) also pull us back onto the Manager's schedule.

Our team has converted most of our emails, SMS and instant messaging to using Slack to communicate. Which is great – when I'm in Manager mode. It is incredibly frustrating when I'm trying to find flow on a task while I'm on the Maker's schedule and Slack messages are coming through thick and fast. Thankfully, the app has the functionality to take you offline when you need to get shit done!

If you have your own business or team, then you could allocate certain days when all of the team will be either on the Maker's or Manager's schedule. For example, Tuesdays and Thursdays could be Maker days – so the entire team has their head down and only very urgent meetings are scheduled.

You will know yourself how much flexibility you have to designate specific days as Maker or Manager. If that's not available to you, then perhaps trying to take the first couple of hours each day to devote to Maker-friendly tasks and then focusing on meetings for the rest of the day might work well.

When he was working on his startup in the early 1990s, Paul Graham unconsciously used to do this. He would work on programming from dinner-time until 3 a.m., as no one could interrupt him at night. Then he would sleep until 11 a.m. and work on what he called 'the business stuff'. He essentially had two work days in one day – one on the Maker's schedule and one on the Manager's schedule.

Monday momentum

The entire success of my week rests on how I spend my Monday.

For example, Monday sets the tone for how I eat for the rest of the week. If I don't have good food prepared for Monday, and for whatever reason I don't eat as well as I would want to, then my motivation to kick-start healthier eating for the rest of the week wanes.

Ditto if I allow a meeting to slip in. No matter how urgent the meeting might be, I feel the impact on my productivity for the entire week afterwards.

If you can, try to make Monday the day that you set the momentum for your week ahead. When we have a Monday that runs smoothly and sees us tick off some chunky items from our to-do list, we sail into Tuesday feeling accomplished and ready to take on the world – spelling success for the rest of the week.

Lynn Taylor, a national workplace expert and author, says that: 'Because you've stepped away for a couple days, these back-to-work mornings are the most memorable for the rest of the week. They influence your mindset in a positive or negative way, depending on what actions you decide to take.'[3]

Meeting buffer time

A very common complaint in our current working climate is 'too many meetings, too little time'. Many of us find that our days are absorbed by meetings, and time at our desk to actually do all the work that we said we'd do in meetings is in scarce supply.

I find this is especially true for those of us who work in large corporates. I have friends employed in these big businesses who have a precious day clear that they're eagerly awaiting so that they can finally work through their bulging to-do list. They step away from their desk for a quick meeting, and on their return they find that the entire day has been booked out by a couple of colleagues.

The net result is that we spend all day in meetings, worrying about all the work we need to get done in tiny windows of time – which means we need to complete it less thoroughly than we'd like, or we work late into the night, or we just never get to it.

Something I've been experimenting with recently is booking in thirty minutes of buffer time after certain meetings. There are regular meetings that I know will require me to work through action points – which involves me sharing some information with the person with whom I met, reviewing some material or looping someone else into a conversation.

A perfect example is my monthly catch-up with our financial controller. Invariably after our meeting, there'll be an Excel spreadsheet of transactions for me to allocate, an email to send to the team with some unknown payments to be identified, or five other similar tasks that take only five minutes, but bank up until our next meeting if I don't address them.

I have started allowing thirty minutes immediately after the finance meeting ends, which I use to tick through these actions – meaning I can move on to the next meeting with a clear head, and I'm not becoming an annoying bottleneck for our financial controller.

Think about what meetings you have regularly that result in an action list – and try to allow some time straight after that meeting to complete those actions. It's an absolute game-changer and you'll feel like a rock star of efficiency once you've done it!

Time blocking tasks

There are a couple of schools of thought on whether or not completing specific tasks should be diarised (assigning specific times of the day for tasks).

Time blocking was created by Georgetown University professor Cal Newport, and is inspired by Parkinson's Law – the idea that any task will expand to the amount of time we allow for it. Time blocking means that we get super-specific about *exactly* what task we'll work on at *exactly* what time during the day.

At the end of each day, Newport spends 15–20 minutes time-blocking the next day and claims that a 40-hour time-blocked week achieves the same as a 60-hour non-time-blocked week.

Personally, I don't time block tasks and instead use my daily to-do list to guide me on what needs to get done. The exception would be if a task is going to take an especially long time, or if it's something about which I've been procrastinating. In either of these cases, I'll book time in to ensure that I get it done – even if it means breaking that mammoth task down into five 'phases', one of which I complete each day of the week.

For my friends in corporate life, booking out time in your calendar to do actual work (aside from meetings, that is) is a great way to protect your time from over-eager colleagues. A meet-in-the-middle solution could be to block out time as 'No meetings please' so that your team knows you have other priorities (i.e. actually getting some work done!) at that time.

Executive assistant Jo Foster tells me that blocking out time in the calendar of the person she's assisting is 'critical' to them actually having some time to do their work – otherwise their time is gradually eaten away by meetings, and their productivity grinds to a halt.

The GRO list

1. Use the Perfect Week template to map out what your ideal week would be. Revisit this each week as you plan your week and inch gradually closer to it as you go.
2. Decide the best time each week for you to have your weekly planning session. Put it in your diary.
3. Figure out the best use of this planning session for you personally, using suggestions in this chapter as a basis.
4. Consider having a day or two each week – or even one morning – that you can devote purely to getting shit done without any other commitments.
5. Aim for Monday momentum, if you can swing it, as part of your week.

CHAPTER 9

Structuring your day

Once we have a good handle on our weeks, our next step is to decide how we want to manage each individual block of twenty-four hours that we have to play with.

In this chapter I will share key principles and structures to help you get the very most out of your day. These tips have already helped many people get organised, though I want to stress that your best daily structure will be what works for you.

I am a big believer in the power of modelling – that is, copying what someone else is doing – because if it's working for them then it could work for me. However, what works for me may not – for whatever reason – be the best approach for you. So we'll also explore how successful people manage their days to give you something of a smorgasbord to build an approach to each day that maximises your capacity and productivity while minimising your stress levels!

The art of the to-do list

Over the years, I've developed a successful to-do list structure. This list has evolved from various iterations, and the version with which I work now is one that I've used every day for the last five years.

In *Remarkability*, I created and shared a number of worksheets that I personally used as part of my visioning, goal-setting and daily planning. Thinking it may be of use to a few people, I included a Word template of how I manage my to-do list.

This template is the most downloaded worksheet from my website – thousands of people are using it to map out their days, and it seems to be working ... Readers tell me that their days are ten times more productive since using the system, and even my own team has adopted it – I simply never realised it was so effective.

One of my mentees, Janine, has a genius approach to making the template work for her. She prints out five copies of it for the week ahead (Monday to Friday), notes the day and date at the top, and jots down her key focuses for each day. This not only gives her a strong blueprint for every day, but a visual for the week ahead as well – which she can then add to as her week progresses and new tasks drop in.

I always work with a paper to-do list, for a couple of reasons. First, writing a paper list makes my action items more tangible than a Word document or digital list app – similar to how paying for something in cash feels more like 'real money' than handing over a card.

Second, nothing compares to ticking off a task when it's been completed. In fact, I'll sometimes write down a task that suddenly popped up after I've done it, just so I can tick it off. Sad, I know!

So, how does it work?

The to-do list structure is split into four distinct sections, which are geared at creating a cascade of priorities for the day ahead.

	Personal task _____
	Personal task _____
	Personal task _____
Friday	
	MIT 1 _____
	MIT 2 _____
	MIT 3 _____
Medium task _____	Small/quick task _____
Medium task _____	Small/quick task _____
Medium task _____	Small/quick task _____
Medium task _____	Small/quick task _____
Medium task _____	Small/quick task _____

How I structure my to-do list each day

Section 1: MITs

In Leo Babauta's book *The Power of Less*, he introduces the concept of MITs. These are Most Important Tasks, the absolutely critical things you need to do on a particular day.

Brian Tracy has a similar concept, which he calls the 'frog'. In his book *Eat That Frog!*, he argues for getting the most difficult thing on your list done first, and suggests that approaching your day in that way is a marker of a 'high performing individual'.

> Apparently, Mark Twain said that if the first thing you do in the morning is eat a live frog, you can go through the rest of the day knowing the worst is behind you.

Your frog is your worst task, and you should do it first thing in the morning. The idea is to tackle your frog, or MITs, first thing in the morning before the demands of the day (kids, emails, colleagues) start to compete for your attention. Then you work on them and work on them until they're completed – not allowing yourself to get pulled into other tasks, conversation or, as Tracy calls it, 'low-value activity' until the frogs are done.

A classic example of low-value activity is clearing our email inboxes. I love entrepreneur Sabri Suby's description of email – he sees it as other people's to-do lists for him; therefore, he ensures that he completes his own to-do list first.

My MITs can generally be broken down into four distinct types of tasks:

1. Tasks that will move the business forward

These are the really big hairy jobs that I know will have an impact on getting us closer to the point we want to be at. That might be writing an opinion piece for a trade media title, planning an upcoming strategy day with the team or following up on conversations with three new business prospects.

2. Something I've been delaying on starting

We'll talk more about procrastination in Chapter 12. I generally find that if I've been putting something off, making that task an MIT forces me to get it done once and for all.

3. Something boring

I absolutely *abhor* process and detail – I need to work really, really hard to motivate myself to undertake tasks in this area. The thought of checking legal contracts or process maps or reviewing accounts quite honestly makes me itchy – the team laugh at how little I seem to make an appearance in our 'Systems & Processes' Slack channel. If so-called 'boring' tasks are not made an MIT, then the chances of me making them a priority are very slim.

4. Something that will take time

If something is going to occupy a significant portion of my day, then it needs to sit within my MITs. If it doesn't, I run the risk of running out of time later in the day and not getting to complete (or even start!) that task. Front-loading our days with the more time-consuming tasks makes sense as we ensure we'll have sufficient time to work on them. Let's also remember that when we know a task is going to take more time, we can easily bump it for something we know we can get done quicker. We are suckers for immediate gratification!

The rule with MITs is that you need to complete them *before* you move on to the following sections. This takes discipline.

It's the easiest thing in the world to skip past an MIT when something further down the list is easier, more exciting or sits within your comfort zone – trust me, I still have to crack down on myself on many days!

> The sense of achievement when you've ticked off your MITs (or your frogs) is fantastic, and sets up buckets of momentum for the rest of the day.

Blogger Alexx Stuart splits her day into two parts. The morning is for what she calls 'have to' work, which involves ticking off her three most important tasks. Then her afternoon is for 'want to' work – that is, the fun tasks that she looks forward to doing.

Section 2: Medium tasks

Once our MITs are ticked off, we tackle our medium tasks. What these are and how long they take will vary from person to person; however, for me tasks in this section tend to take approximately fifteen minutes to complete.

Examples of medium tasks might be reviewing progress on a client strategy with one of the team, making an admin call (e.g. to our phone provider or insurance company) or completing the action points from a meeting held the day before.

Section 3: Quick tasks

Park speedy little jobs in this section – things you know you can knock over in less than three minutes. This could be following up on an email, calling someone to confirm a meeting the next day or sending a text.

I use this section to capture those 'oh, must do that' thoughts; popping them down on my list means they're out of my brain and I keep my mind focused on the task at hand.

When I get 'Lorraine when you have a sec ... ' requests from the team, I jot that person's name down in this section so that I'll remember to get back to them when I've completed the other tasks on my list.

Section 4: Personal tasks

This last section is a neat little home for all that personal life admin that each of us needs to complete on a day-to-day basis. It might be changing our home energy provider, booking cinema tickets for that night or picking up a birthday gift for our mum. Generally these personal tasks come at the end of the cascade of priorities for me, although if one is urgent then I'll tackle it earlier in the day.

Note: If you're not currently working or running a business, you may find that this section is redundant. As I write this chapter, for example, I'm on the entrepreneur's version of maternity leave (i.e. trying to step back from the business) after the arrival of our first baby. Baby admin is featuring both in my MITs and my Medium Tasks sections, and I've hardly been using the Personal Tasks section.

There are a few reasons I think this to-do list approach is so effective:

1. It creates a visual 'waterfall' of cascading priorities, so we're prioritising our time and energy according to what's actually most important.
2. It clearly separates the more time-consuming tasks from the less time-consuming ones. When we have one big to-do list with each task listed on a similar footing, we think every task is as important as all the others – when in reality 'writing strategy for client X' will take four hours but 'text Sarah to confirm coffee tomorrow' will take twenty seconds.

3. If we follow the flow, then the tasks we don't get to by the end of the day shouldn't be the mission-critical ones and can be transferred over to the next day's list for completion.

You can get the to-do list template as a free printable download from my website – lorrainemurphy.com.au – and there are also pads of the lists available for purchase.

Successful to-do lists

I love observing how other people manage their to-do lists, as I find everyone's approach is unique to them. However, successful people are the most interesting to me as I'm constantly on the hunt for little hacks that they're using to get ahead which I can shamelessly incorporate into how I manage my days.

Barbara Corcoran, a *Shark Tank* investor, breaks down her daily to-do list into three distinct phases:

1. Calls – typically two to three calls.
2. Review – items she needs to look over or approve.
3. Projects – actions related to the various businesses in which she invests; this area of her list is where she says the 'gold' is, as it makes her money.

I find this approach interesting as it's actually quite counter-intuitive to the approach we've just walked through. Rather than focusing on heavy-duty action items upfront, Barbara instead knocks over some quick wins in terms of calls and approvals before knuckling down to the money-making stuff. It clearly works for her and might also suit you.

Barbara is also a big fan of the paper to-do list (like me). Having tried various online to-do lists, she says: 'The delete button will never give you the kicks that crossing off tasks will give you.' A woman after my own heart!

Jim McCann, author and founder of 1-800-Flowers Inc, has a number of lists that he maintains: a 'things I have to do today' list, a more general to-do list, a projects list and a long-term ideas list. In his words: 'Lists help you look at how you're spending your time. It's easy to be busy and a lot harder to be effective.' Also someone after my own heart!

TV personality and founder of Swiish.com, Sally Obermeder, maintains a rather comprehensive to-do list, which lives in a Word document. She breaks it down according to the areas of her life – *The Daily Edition*, SWIISH, Home, Socials, etc. She then breaks down each of these areas into sub-categories – for example, underneath SWIISH are sections for the website, books, shop, product development, publicity, strategy. This document stays open all day and she updates it throughout the day.

The daily time plan

Another tool I like to use to keep myself on track is a daily time plan. Warning: this is stupidly basic! However, it helps me to have a visual plan of what tasks I'll do when. I also like the satisfaction of ticking off each item on my time plan as I do it.

Most of my days are governed by whatever meetings and appointments are in my calendar, but on other days – like when I'm working at home or having a no-meeting day – I like to map out in the morning how the day ahead is going to play out.

This captures my MITs, email time, break times and chunks of time to deal with reacting to requests. I'll even specify what meals I'll be eating so I can look forward to them!

So it might look like this:

9.00 a.m.	MIT 1: Book writing
11.00 a.m.	Break – smoothie
11.15 a.m.	MIT 2: Review client strategy
11.45 a.m.	MIT 3: Call lawyer re contract
12.00 p.m.	Lunch (chicken leftovers)
12.30 p.m.	Email time
1.30 p.m.	Walk
2.00 p.m.	Medium tasks
3.00 p.m.	Admin/getting back to people
3.30 p.m.	Any other tasks
4.30 p.m.	Prep dinner (vegetable soup)
5.15 p.m.	Walk to yoga
5.30 p.m.	Yoga class
6.45 p.m.	Home & shower
7.00 p.m.	Food prep & eat dinner
8.00 p.m.	Watch a show with Wade
9.30 p.m.	Bed
10.00 p.m.	Sleep

A note on discipline

I know, I know, I know. I am banging on about this mental muscle constantly. Sticking rigidly to a structured to-do list or a daily time plan is not easy – particularly when the tasks we have to do are tasks that we just don't enjoy or we've been procrastinating about them for weeks already.

It is critical that we persist through the feelings of inertia or absolute boredom and stick with the plan that we map out for ourselves at the start of the day (or, even better, at the end of the previous day). Practice makes permanent, and I promise you that the more you work on sticking to your plan, the easier it will get.

The GRO list

1. Download the to-do list template from my website. If it works for you, invest in a notepad of to-do lists.
2. Commit to working with the template for at least two weeks.
3. If you need added motivation to stick with it, use it in conjunction with the Weekly Habits Scorecard and give yourself a reward each week that you successfully work with the system.
4. Consider using a daily time plan if you'd like to give yourself additional structure.

CHAPTER 10

Conquering distractions

You don't need me to tell you that we live in what is most certainly the most distraction-rich society that has ever existed. Terrifyingly, this trend shows no sign of abating and it feels, to me anyway, that our poor brains have to work harder and harder to keep up with the sheer volume of distractions coming our way.

Why are we so distracted?

I read an article recently that quoted a University of Melbourne academic, Dan Woodman. Woodman has identified that people born between 1977 and 1983 are currently something of a segue between Generation X and Milliennials.[1] They grew up without ubiquitous technology until around their university years, yet were still young enough to adopt technology fully into their lives.

The article suggested that they be deemed a 'microgeneration' and be dubbed 'Xennials'. Now I don't know if that's altogether necessary; however, I do feel privileged that I was born in 1982 and therefore experienced life before technology became a centrepoint of our lives.

Having access to information at our fingertips means that we are used to immediate gratification. If I'm out for drinks with a friend and we're trying to remember the name of the actor who plays a character in a TV show, we don't discuss it for twenty minutes. Instead, one of us – or more likely both of us – will pull out our smartphones and we race to see who can find the actor's name first. This is standard for life AT (After Tech).

Look at how we watch TV. In the past, we would eagerly await a certain night of the week as that's when our favourite TV show was on, and we accepted that ad breaks were part of the deal.

Now I don't even own a TV. All my shows and movies are watched on my laptop. I can't remember the last time I saw an ad break – never mind sat through one. I am so used to consuming content on demand that when Netflix only releases one episode a week, I feel cheated as I can't immediately move on to the next episode.

I cannot sit through an entire hour of a show without checking my phone once, and often do a social media post about what I'm watching. The age of the second screen is well and truly here.

When I was working as an account director in a small PR agency just eight years ago, I could only access my email inbox from my desktop computer at the office. My clients called me possibly once a week on my mobile; all other calls went to the phone on my desk. I primarily used my mobile phone for calls and texts, and occasionally checked social media on it – my Facebook and Twitter surfing normally took place on my lunch breaks ... at my desk.

Just writing that paragraph, I am absolutely blown away at how dramatically the advances in technology in just eight years have impacted my day-to-day life.

Now I don't even have a desk phone, as everyone calls me on my mobile. In fact, we have just one desktop phone across our entire team – which rings probably twice a week – and we use our mobiles exclusively for outgoing calls.

My smartphone is hooked up to my emails, so I can access them anywhere in the world at any time.

I rarely use Facebook on my computer; instead, I check it multiple times a day on my phone.

Newer social media channels like Instagram and YouTube have gained prominence and increasingly sophisticated features. With the advent of Instagram Stories, I don't just post once daily on social media, but several times a day.

I receive direct messages through each of the channels, and I exchange text, video and photos with friends and family via those channels – as well as 'old school' SMS, WhatsApp and Viber. In a (thankfully successful) effort to cut down the volume of internal emails, I communicate with my team on Slack.

As I write this chapter, 'walkie-talkie' apps like Voxer are taking off so that, rather than investing time in making a call or typing a text, I can simply record a voice message and hit send to a recipient.

Many of us struggle with staying on top of our emails (more on that soon); however, it's important that we acknowledge these various platforms and apps for what they are: another inbox to manage.

Just eight years ago I had four 'inboxes' to respond to: SMS, business email, personal email and Facebook.

Fast forward to today and I have eleven: SMS, business email, personal email, Facebook, Instagram, Twitter, Snapchat, WhatsApp, Viber, Voxer and Slack. If we put this in a business context, can you imagine the resistance a manager would get if they almost tripled the workload of one of their team members? Mutiny would be imminent!

My working life is no longer centred on a desk with four legs in a stationary office that I need to travel to and from every day. Never again will I walk out of the office at 5.30 p.m. and not reconnect until 9 a.m. the next morning – that's a whole 15.5 hours to unplug! This has huge ramifications for how our brains are functioning. They quite simply never get to switch off. My desk now lives in my smartphone – which is rarely outside of the same room as me.

We are more available than we have ever been – which makes it incredibly difficult to define and protect boundaries around our time and headspace. This lack of boundaries due to our constant connectedness has extended to the physical world as well.

While I was in university, I had a few receptionist roles. One was at a printing company, and the phone never, ever rang between 1 and 2 p.m. That's because people were either off having their lunch break or were conscious that maybe the people at the company I worked at would be on their lunch break, and it was an unwritten rule that you just didn't phone over that sixty minutes.

It would never even cross my mind now not to call someone between 1 and 2 p.m. – I automatically assume that everyone is available at any time of day. Even if it's too early in the morning or too late in the evening to phone someone, I'll send them a text or email that – depending on how connected they choose to be – they can access 24/7.

A team works very differently today from how it did ten years ago. Back then, a team probably had a weekly meeting to check in on progress on a certain client or project. That was the team's window each week to ask any questions they might have of their manager – and so get their feedback on an idea or have them review some material.

Now a team doesn't need to wait until that meeting – they'll send a message to their manager on email or via Slack and the functionality also allows them to upload documents for the manager to review.

The communication loop is getting smaller and smaller in direct correlation to how sophisticated technology is becoming – meaning we're working faster and faster.

The pace that technology is dictating in our lives, and the sheer volume of information coming our way, have a number of consequences:

1. Our brains are unable to focus on just one thing anymore.
2. We are more available to others than we have ever been.
3. *We're in a quagmire of distraction.*

Why are distractions so damaging?

We can have our morning routine and evening routine planned down to the most minute detail, have a well thought-out and organised to-do list, and a beautifully colour-coded calendar. 'I'm getting remarkably organised!' we tell ourselves.

Yet it all goes to absolute shit if we cannot protect ourselves from the perils of distractions.

Distractions – put terribly bluntly – fuck any hope we might have of feeling organised. And they fuck it up big time.

Why is that? Let's explore the perils of distraction in more detail ...

1. They're deliciously sinful

Distractions are like the pastries left over from someone else's meeting in the office. I know they'll taste really, really good. However, it's 11 a.m. on a Wednesday and I know I don't really need to eat one. I'm not hungry and I'm pretty proud of the healthy food I've had already that day. I've got a kick-ass lunch waiting in the fridge: leftovers from the delicious dinner I had the night before.

I eat a pastry anyway.

It doesn't taste as good as I thought it would. I have a sugar crash precisely twenty-five minutes later. I'm not hungry for my lunch when it's time to eat it. I'm just annoyed with myself.

Distractions are exactly the same as the leftover office pastries. They hold a promise of something exciting or fun, and a diversion from whatever task we have at hand. Ultimately, they are empty of any substance and we're annoyed at ourselves for indulging when we do. Think of Adam, Eve, the apple and the Garden of Eden.

2. They can be a rabbit hole

I find that distractions have a tunnel-like tendency. I might open Instagram to send a quick direct message to someone; however, I somehow find myself on the Discover tab and all of a sudden I'm twenty posts back on some random person's page – someone I will likely never meet and probably don't necessarily care to meet.

Or one of the team asks me for two minutes to answer a quick question. I answer the question, but ten minutes later we're still talking and have jumped across five different conversation topics and we each have four action points added to our to-do lists.

3. They create refocus time as well

We need to factor in not just the time taken to deal with a distraction, but also the time required to get back into the task we interrupted to address it. For example, I spend ten minutes in that conversation with one of my team, but it takes me a good fifteen minutes to refocus on writing the client strategy I had been working on before I got distracted.

A University of California study found that it takes an average of twenty-three minutes and fifteen seconds to get back into a task following an interruption. Let's say on a very good day we get just five interruptions ... I'll leave you to do the maths on that.

4. They're demotivating

Just like the pastry eating, when we allow a distraction to take us off track, we get shitty with ourselves.

Up until I ate the pastry, I was on track with eating well for the day and was congratulating myself on the nutritious breakfast I had taken the time to cook myself, the green smoothie and the veggie-packed lunch awaiting my eating pleasure in the fridge.

After I've eaten the pastry, I'm telling myself that I'm greedy, I have no willpower and I've fucked my healthy eating for the day now. It's also more than likely that when some sweets magically appear on one of the team's desks later in the afternoon that I'll have some – as I've already fallen off the healthy wagon today.

My friend Melissa Ambrosini talks about the social media rabbit hole – you know, when you plan to check social media quickly, and forty minutes later you're still aimlessly scrolling? She says she feels 'gross' after it. I so get that feeling!

5. They're contagious

Distractions not only take us off course, but often affect the people around us too.

I might allow myself to open an email from a friend when I should in fact be reviewing a legal contract. The email has a funny sixty-second cat video, which I watch and giggle along to. *Of course* the three people sitting around me want to know what I'm laughing at, so the email gets circulated and, rather than just me distracting myself, now three other people are also distracted.

Roughly calculating the time to down tools, check the email, open the video and watch it, that's two minutes per person. Add in twenty-three minutes for all four of us to get refocused on what we're supposed to be doing, and that takes the time cost of the distraction up to one hour and forty minutes.

How we can combat distractions

As I've already said, distractions are simply too tempting. I've found that I cannot trust myself when they're around, so putting in place some systems and rules is essential to prevent them taking me off course. I still get distracted, but I have put in place safeguards to protect myself from them as much as humanly possible. Here we go ...

Guard your time fiercely

There is a reason why we have worked through your ideal week, ideal day and how you want to approach your to-do list each day. I also wanted to share the concept of paying yourself first with your time before we hit the topic of distractions.

It is utterly essential that we each decide first and foremost how *we* want to spend our time. If we don't, then other people will decide for us. And once that power is handed over, it becomes increasingly difficult to pull it back again.

With the chaos of distractions that surround us, we need to be an absolute tiger – a Get Shit Done Tiger – when it comes to protecting our time so that we can get the shit done that we need to get done.

It is down to each of us as individuals to draw the boundaries when it comes to distractions – both those we seek out ourselves (like social media or performing unimportant tasks around the house instead of the big one we *should* be doing) and the ones that others send our way (interruptions in person, emails, phone calls).

We will all get pulled off course at some stage in the day by an incoming request from someone – be that in person, via a phone call or in an email. However, when those distractions become the norm, we only have ourselves to blame when we have spent the day pandering to other people's to-do lists and not tending to our own.

> The key to protecting our time is to actually give ourselves something to protect.

If we're floating through each day with no clear plan, then we're wide open to being distracted. This is where the to-do list, daily time plan and embedded morning/evening routines come in. We are creating a structure that we value and want to protect.

We also have some recourse when people interrupt us – rather than being constantly available, we are genuinely engaged in a specific task and so cannot be distracted right now.

Next time a distraction comes your way, picture a Get Shit Done Tiger in your mind and protect your time fiercely.

Communicate when you're working on something

When you're getting stuck into your MITs or another key task, make sure people know that you're heading into Do Not Disturb mode and can't be interrupted.

When they forget and interrupt you anyway, remind them politely that you're still working on that task. Jot their name down in the Quick Tasks section of your to-do list so they know they're in the queue for your attention, and then crack on with what you were doing.

When I need 100 per cent focus, I'll get some power ballads playing on my phone, tell the team I'm heading into Mariah/Whitney/Beyoncé Land and put my headphones in.

Work out a system that flags when you're not to be disturbed, and work with the people around you to ensure that system is respected.

Office furniture purveyors Steelcase plan this year to release a desk with built-in red and green lights so users can clearly communicate their availability for interruptions – similar to the red/green light system in multi-storey carparks. When the light is red, it means steer clear. There are several plug-in solutions already available on the market.

I love the simple solution adopted by a Coca-Cola exec, who wanted to maintain his open-door policy, but was fed up with colleagues constantly wandering in and interrupting him. He established his own signalling system – if he was wearing a red Coca-Cola baseball cap, he was engrossed in a task and couldn't be interrupted unless it was for something urgent.

Get comfortable saying no

Many of us would rather keep everyone else happy than keep ourselves happy by actually getting the things we need to do done. We'll take the phone call, say yes to 'Can I have a quick chat with you?' (note: it's never quick), and respond to text messages immediately so we don't keep the other person waiting.

A woman attended a bootcamp event I ran earlier this year and she said that the number one block to her being on top of life was the constant interruptions from her team. She estimated that they disturbed her *at least* twenty times every day – to the extent where she was considering working from home for a few days a week just so she could get some work done.

It is a key step in your getting remarkably organised journey to get comfortable with the NO word.

Remember the need to guard your time like the Get Shit Done Tiger. Also remember that until you respect your own time – and protect it – no one else will either.

Turn off all notifications

I worked for a while with someone whose notification habit was out of control.

I would sit next to her to review some work on her laptop and notifications would pop up constantly in the corner of her screen – one every time she received an email (across three inboxes), one every time something happened on Twitter and ditto for Facebook, one every time something was updated in our business Dropbox folder and fuck knows how many others.

There wasn't just an onscreen notification; her computer would make a noise every time – and to make it even worse, her phone was also hooked up to notifications so there was a cacophony of both noises and things flashing up on two screens. All. The. Time.

It blew my mind how she actually got anything done. Generally, she was pretty on top of her work; however, her general demeanour was one of being a bit frazzled and I constantly wondered how much more capacity and potential she would have if she didn't have these micro-distractions coming her way incessantly.

There is real-life research showing that getting constant notifications can trigger stress. For example, in a survey of nearly 2000 workers in the United Kingdom, the London-based Future Work Centre found that email notifications were linked to higher feelings of anxiety.

Researchers at the University of British Columbia asked 124 students and professors to check their email frequently for one week. The next week, they only checked their email three times per day and disabled all notifications. When time spent looking at email was restricted, the participants reported lower stress levels and higher feelings of positivity.

We have already discussed in detail how physical clutter can hamper our ability to get organised and to feel we're getting shit done day to day. What we need to remember is that notifications – of any sort – also represent clutter, this time mental clutter.

As a Life Hacker article[2] states, when we have notifications coming in, our brains don't get a chance to fully enter creative flow or process experiences. When our brains have too much on their neural plate, they divide their power. The result of this is that we become rubbish at filtering information, switching quickly between tasks and keeping a strong working memory – all pretty key things to keep us on track day to day, don't you reckon?

We must recognise these notifications for what they are: micro-tasks in their own right. When we have notifications coming in, we are effectively dealing with incoming tasks – and worse, we need to switch rapidly between tasks. Remember that it takes twenty-three minutes to fully click back into the task we were originally doing before the interruption, and the true impact of these notifications becomes terrifyingly apparent.

Gloria Mark, Professor in the Department of Informatics at the University of California, oversaw a study exploring the impact of task switching.[3] An experiment was carried out in which people did a typical office task, answering a batch of emails. In one condition, they were not interrupted. In another condition, the group was interrupted with phone calls and instant messaging. Using a NASA workload scale that measures various dimensions of stress, the scientists found that people scored significantly higher when interrupted. They had higher levels of stress, frustration, mental effort, feelings of time pressure and mental workload. There was no significant difference in the number of errors between those who were interrupted and those who were not.

Something absolutely fascinating that the experiments uncovered was that when people were not interrupted, they worked more slowly. As Professor Mark explained, 'You know you're going to be continually interrupted so you compensate by working faster, but the cost of that is stress.'

I have no notifications at all on either my phone or computers. If I want to know if I have new emails, I have to open my email inbox to find out. If I want to know what's happening on Instagram, I need to open the app and find out. As a result, the only time my phone makes a noise is when I get a text message or phone call, and my computer makes no noise at all.

For the purposes of illustrating my own point in this chapter, I had planned to switch on all of my smartphone notifications for a 48-hour period (across business email, Instagram, Facebook, Snapchat, Slack and Twitter), and to total how many notifications I received.

I couldn't do it. I knew that doing so would drive me insane, and would stymie any chance I had of getting work done. At such an important time (I was re-entering the business after maternity leave), I simply couldn't undertake such a major block to my productivity.

These micro-distractions are a certified killer of any organisational potential we might have and – thankfully – they are completely unnecessary.

Schedule social media time

Social media is the ultimate 21st century distraction.

The various platforms offer us hours of whiling away the time in a completely pointless way. I once heard TV described as 'chewing gum for the brain' and I'm convinced that social media has taken out the top spot on that front now. Social media is an even more slippery slope than TV, however, because – unlike a 32-inch screen television – social media is accessible no matter where we are via our smartphones.

I have had a love/hate relationship with social media over the last few years.

Love because its existence meant that I was able to build a very successful business that helps social influencers and brands work together, I've founded wonderful relationships with people I wouldn't have met outside of social media and it's a source of great ideas.

Hate as it occupies an enormous amount of time, it's far too easy to slip into a black hole of scrolling, and I have definitely experienced times when I felt addicted to it.

One way I have reined in my use of social media was to give myself incentives to reduce my time on it to twice a day. I used the Weekly Habits Scorecard mentioned in Chapter 5 to keep myself accountable, and found that since then the time I have spent online has been significantly reduced.

Now I generally find that my time on social media is contained to certain times of the day – mostly after my Miracle Morning and in the evenings after dinner; however, I will dip in and out quickly at various times of the day.

If you, like me, struggle with social media overtaking more important priorities in your life, then think about some steps you can take to reduce the time you spend online – and wonder at how much more organised you feel!

Don't accept calls if the time doesn't suit

The evening before I wrote this chapter, Wade drove to Newcastle for a meeting. He spent the 1.5 hours in the car there and back batching his phone calls – meaning the otherwise 'dead time' driving was actually productive. His plan was to arrive home at 5.45 p.m., change his clothes and head to the gym.

Two people who he had tried to call on his way to Newcastle (six hours earlier) phoned him back as he pulled up outside our house – so he spent twenty minutes on the phone to one of them while sitting in the car, then called the second person back and spoke to him for thirty minutes. The result was that he didn't walk in the front door until 6.45 p.m. and his window to get to the gym was gone ... and he was rather cranky.

Getting to the gym was a key priority for him this week: he had designed a day-by-day work-out program and he was pissed off that he didn't manage to keep that commitment with himself.

What I found interesting was that he had tried to call both these people that morning, but they hadn't called him back until that evening – as earlier in the day (for whatever reason) hadn't suited *their* schedules. When they eventually phoned him back, he felt obligated to answer their calls at the expense of what was an important activity for him.

Generally, we'll make a phone call at a time that suits *us*; however, the other person does have a choice as to whether they engage in a conversation with us when we call.

The person we're calling will do one of four things when their phone screen flashes:

1. Answer the phone.
2. Miss the call as their phone is on silent or they're away from it.
3. See the call coming through, not answer it and call back later.
4. See the call coming through, not answer it and don't call back later.

Most often, I will fall into the camp of Number 3. I will only answer a call if it's coming at a time when I'm not doing something else – otherwise I'll make a note (mental or on my to-do list) to call the person back when I'm finished the task at hand.

For me, phone calls are one of the worst distractions. I can't control when they come in (unlike me choosing to while away ten minutes on Facebook) and I have no idea what they hold in store. For example, if I'm head down on business strategy and the bank calls about setting up some new accounts, I'm pulled into a very different headspace and it's even more difficult to get back into the original task I was doing.

I realised a few years ago that just because my phone is ringing, it doesn't mean I automatically need to answer it. This has been a gamechanger in terms of managing the distraction of phone calls. Of course, the key is to actually call people back – otherwise it's just rude!

> It's important that we remember that we always have a choice about whether we take a call or not.

I suggest you make your time a priority and get comfortable with letting calls go to voicemail when you're in GSD (Get Shit Done) mode. Even better, put your phone on silent and have it face down so you can't see calls coming through – which is exactly what my phone is doing as I type this line right now!

If you're someone who needs to make a lot of phone calls for their job (and I'm not one of them), it might be helpful to try to batch your calls together into one hour or a couple of hours a day. That way, you can focus fully on making them, and you also have time designated to return any calls that you may have missed outside of that time.

Pause your inbox

When I'm on a mission to get my emails cleared, I'll generally start from the top and work my way down – blasting out responses one by one until eventually I'm at zero (BEST FEELING EVA!!!).

I have found that a dangerous distraction is when the people I'm replying to are also online and they start replying to my replies in real time. I then jump back up to the top of my inbox and reply back to them – a) as I can catch them while they're online, and b) because I've already given brain power to the question/topic they raised in their email, so it feels much easier to respond to their new email than get stuck into an unrelated older email.

The problem with addressing the 'real-time' emails at the same time as older ones still awaiting my first reply is that it's a never-ending cycle. I'll reply to them, they reply back to me – all the while the backlog isn't getting cleared.

Gmail has a super-smart plug-in called 'Pause Inbox', which does exactly what it says on the tin. It will temporarily hold off on allowing any new emails to hit my inbox, giving me the headspace to deal with the old stuff first.

The GRO list

1. Identify what the three biggest distractions are for you day to day – what is consistently taking you off track from the stuff you're supposed to be doing?
2. Against each of these distractions, identify one action you can take to conquer it.
3. Take one distraction at a time and practise minimising the impact it's having on your ability to stay organised. I suggest making it a focus of your Weekly Habits Scorecard in Chapter 5 so you can reward yourself for staying on track.
4. Make it another habit to tell other people around you when you're in Get Shit Done mode.
5. Turn off all notifications on all your devices. Yes – ALL of them.

6. If social media is your thing, ask yourself honestly whether it's taking up too much of your time – and put a plan in place to be more intentional with it.

7. Don't feel you need to answer your phone just because it's ringing. You don't.

8. Channel your Get Shit Done Tiger! Protect your time fiercely.

CHAPTER 11

Outsourcing

Outsourcing is a term borrowed from the corporate world, that refers to taking a function of a business and having it looked after by an external company. When we apply this to our personal lives, outsourcing involves taking things that we normally have to do in our day-to-day lives, and giving them to someone else to do.

The first public mention of personal outsourcing was by AJ Jacobs of *Esquire* in 2005. His article was a humorous look at just how much of your life could be run by a team of virtual assistants. The article was – of course – written by an outsourced team!

Personal outsourcing has become pretty damn trendy in recent years, to the extent that an entire industry is thriving off the backs of time-pressed individuals needing a dig-out with both their working and personal lives.

In fact, Phil Ruthven, chairman of business information analyst firm IBISWorld, claims that about one-third of all Australian household activities are now outsourced.[1] The interweb has made it possible for just about anyone to become a freelancer these days, and in the United States there are 53 million freelance workers. It's estimated that the global online workforce generates between $1 billion and $2 billion annually.

There are likely a multitude of reasons why this is the case; however, I've got a couple of theories of my own.

First, the traditional model of community and family that previous generations experienced is sadly the exception rather than the rule today.

In the past, we would have had a lot more support from the broader community network around us. Between parents, siblings, extended family, neighbours, churches, sporting clubs and social interest groups, we effectively had a small army of people to help us get shit done. When my great-grandmother or any of her siblings had a baby, a maiden aunt would go and stay with the family for the first few months of the baby's life to help the parents (let's be honest – the mum).

My own large family in Ireland still operates like this to a certain extent. As I write, I'm back in Dublin having travelled from Sydney to celebrate my sister's wedding. Having witnessed multiple weddings being planned in Australia, I was blown away by how much my sister was able to outsource to family.

A cousin altered the dress, four aunts prepared the wedding cakes, her new husband's sister made signs and photo boards, multiple people shopped for and transported wedding items, an uncle ferried guests between the wedding reception venue and the after-party venue, a cousin did my sister's hair and make-up for the second night of celebrations ... the list goes on. If we were to calculate the actual value of this help in terms of what it would have cost to pay external suppliers, it would run into the thousands of dollars.

I realised while seeing the wedding come together that the absence of this kind of support in most modern people's lives has a big impact on the workload that each of us carries. By workload, I don't just mean business or career – I also mean the work of living day to day: caring for kids, grocery shopping, boring life admin and so on.

Just after our daughter was born, my mother came to stay with us in Sydney. We were under quite a bit of time pressure to get a passport for our little girl as she needed to travel to Ireland at just six weeks old. This necessitated getting her birth certificate first, which involved pulling together various official documents and a visit to the registry office to get it moving through the system as soon as possible. We then needed to go back to the registry office to collect the birth certificate in order to shave off the couple of days required for a postal delivery.

Once we had the birth certificate in hand, we had two trips to the passport office to check two different passport photos. If anyone reading has tried to get a photo of a newborn that ticks all the ridiculous boxes required by the passport office, you'll feel my pain on this one!

To get to the point where we had a completed passport form and a photo that would pass the scrutiny of the passport officials, roughly fifteen hours were required – most of which my mum took on, thankfully. Had my mum not been in town, much of that fifteen hours would have fallen to myself and Wade.

The fact is that most of us are living in a situation where

we have little to no family nearby who we can lean on for this kind of support, and – if you're like myself and Wade – friends whose plates are full dealing with their own life workloads and aren't in a position to give us a dig out.

If one person has, say, even ten people with whom they can share their workload, between friends, family and neighbours, the overall impact is a hell of a lot less to do and wayyyy less stress. As the saying goes, 'Many hands make light work.'

The result for those of us who don't have access to all these hands is that we're increasingly stressed, which creates perfect conditions for an outsourcing industry to take off.

I also believe that my generation and the generations immediately on either side of it are trying to achieve a hell of a lot more than those who went before us. Wade's grandfather ran a successful plumbing business in Frankston, Victoria, which employed about fifteen staff and enabled him to set up a pretty comfortable life for his wife and family.

Fifty years later and Wade is building his own business. He employs thirteen people, and the team grows to forty at certain points of the year. The difference between Wade and his grandfather is that Wade isn't content with that. He wants his business to grow globally, and invests hours per week on strategy, sales, leadership and research to ensure that happens.

Accessibly priced air travel means that Wade was able to visit seven countries for business in just the last twelve months, while technology enables him to have instant contact with his team all around the world. The result is that he can have much grander aspirations than his grandfather could ever have had in his generation.

This extends across all of us – as a rule, we are trying to achieve a lot more than our grandparents, and probably our parents, ever did. In fact, I don't even think *achievement* and *goals* were things that my grandmother considered. Her focus was on raising nine kids and she ran a succession of small businesses locally in order to achieve that. It was about survival and making do, rather than global domination.

Many of my peers' mothers and grandmothers have told them that they're glad they weren't born into the modern era in which we find ourselves today, as the demands on contemporary women are too great.

> We – men, women, boys and girls – are undertaking a hell of a lot more than any previous generation would or could have, and we're running ourselves ragged as a result.

A small-town restaurateur could probably easily manage having twenty people for dinner each night, with just one chef and waiting on tables themselves. If, however, they want to feed 100 people, that requires a few more chefs, a team of well-organised wait staff, a restaurant manager, and tech solutions to manage bookings and orders.

Many of us are trying to run a 100-person restaurant on our own. And can you imagine the Google reviews that restaurant would be getting?

You cannot do everything.

Well, you can try. However, my bet is that life would be a hell of a lot easier and more efficient if you strategically drafted in extra help.

High value versus low value

Our journey into outsourcing starts with identifying which tasks in your life are high value and which are low value. You'll likely have some that fall in between on the spectrum, but we'll look at the extremities of it first.

A high-value task is one that delivers the most bang for your buck for the time you invest in it. Think of it as return on investment (ROI). For an hour spent on a high-value task, you will likely get high ROI. Conversely, a low-value task will fall pretty short on ROI.

A low-value task does not mean that something isn't worth doing – it simply means that it's likely we can find someone else to look after it so that we can focus our time and energy on our high-value stuff.

Take my business as an example. A high-value activity for me would be spending an hour writing an opinion piece for a trade media website. This work is good for me to spend time on. First, it boosts our profile as a business. Second, it helps us secure revenue. Third, it's work that I am uniquely placed to do. And lastly, it's work that comes easily to me as it plays to my strengths.

Writing this book is a big project to undertake, particularly as much of it has been done while I've been pregnant and with a newborn baby. I love researching interesting studies and statistics while I'm writing; however, I needed to be very judicious about how I approached this book in order to meet the deadlines from my publisher. I decided that I alone could write the book, but I could find someone to support me with research and coordinating the interviews.

Enter stage left my wonderful book assistant, Jo! I write a chapter and make notes as I go, then email the chapter to Jo. She fills in the gaps and emails it back to me, and I weave her interesting findings into the chapter. For me to do the research myself would have added significantly to the time required to complete this book, so outsourcing the tasks that were not critical for me to manage made perfect sense.

I spend my time doing the highest value work on the book – that is, the planning, writing and editing – while Jo looks after the work that is lower in value to me – the research and coordinating interviewees. Her thoroughness means that my mind and time are freed up to focus on writing.

High-value tasks will generally tick one or more of these three boxes:

1. They make you money.
2. They get you closer to your goals.
3. You are the only person, or one of the most relevant people, to complete them: it's a unique skillset to you, or you hold certain relationships, or it plays to your strengths.

Conversely, low-value tasks will generally tick one or more of these three boxes:

1. They don't make you money.
2. They do not move you towards your goals.
3. A number of other people could complete them.

I'll give you some examples from my life.

High-value tasks in The Remarkables Group are:

1. strategy time with my business partner and team
2. quality time with key clients
3. writing thought-leadership pieces.

All three of these tasks tick all three high-value boxes, in that they make us money, move us closer to our goals and I'm one of the most relevant people to do them.

Low-value tasks in The Remarkables Group are:

1. reconciling our accounts
2. writing process documents
3. clearing my email inbox.

None of these ticks any of the three high-value boxes. By spending time on these tasks, I am not making us money, I am not moving closer to my goals and I certainly am not the most relevant person to do them (with the exception of my emails, which are a necessary evil).

Let's look at my home life now.

High-value tasks in the home are:

1. taking care of our daughter
2. doing the weekly meal plan
3. shopping for great food.

Low value tasks in the home are:

1. cleaning the house
2. low-scale DIY.

My goals include having a happy, safe and healthy baby and also being the healthiest and strongest I can be. I can knock out a meal plan and shopping list in ten minutes, whereas it takes Wade three times as long to complete the same task. Technically, someone else could go grocery shopping, but I'm good at it and I enjoy doing it each week. I am my daughter's mother, so that's one task I can't outsource – nor would I want to!

In contrast, the house cleaning is something that a much wider scope of individuals can complete – and complete to a much higher standard than I would. Therefore, it makes sense to outsource those tasks so that I can focus my time on the ones that are high value to our home.

Ditto for low-scale DIY such as hanging pictures (remember that old stone in my shoe?) – it doesn't make sense for me to spend time learning how to do that, buying the relevant tools and hanging frames when there are talented individuals out there who specialise in that very thing.

Take some time to consider what tasks you perform day to day, and start to identify them as sitting in the high-value or low-value camp. I've created an Outsourcing Matrix worksheet to help you do this, which you can download from my website.

This sheet guides you through the main tasks you do in your business or career day to day, and also in your home. It asks you to allocate a score to each one, creating a ladder of tasks so you can visually see which tasks it would make sense for you to outsource and which you should complete yourself.

The outsourcing golden rule

Once you have a handle on what your high-value versus low-value tasks are, you should have a good idea of the tasks you should be starting to hand over to others.

I'm going to share with you now the handiest tool I have come across in helping me choose what to outsource. And it's really very simple.

> First, we set an hourly rate for ourselves, based on us doing high-value tasks. Then if we can find someone else to do a low-value task for less than that, we outsource it.

That's it! Easy!

When I started my business, I set my hourly rate at $200. This was based on pretty much sweet eff all – it just felt like a good number to start with. No one ever actually *paid* me $200 per hour.

Now I've set my hourly rate at $500. A pretty sweet (yet non-existent) pay rise! The reason I've increased it is that my business is a lot more successful and established than when I was just starting it. Now that we have a certain level of success, each hour I spend on my business can deliver even more ROI – in terms of getting me and the business closer to our goals, but also the enjoyment I get from that hour.

I also have a lot more commitments competing for my time than I did five years ago, including my 'other' business of public speaking and writing books like this, not to mention my sweet little girl. Therefore – whenever possible – I need to focus my time on the very top end of the high-value ladder.

Having this fictional hourly rate means that I can very quickly decide whether or not I should outsource a task. It makes absolutely no sense for me to spend an hour writing a process manual when I could outsource that to a professional to do for $100 an hour.

No one is going to pay me $500 to have an hour with our daughter; however, it helps me prioritise my time when I know I can pay someone $100 to spend that hour writing a process manual so I can spend that time with her.

The trickiest part of this rule is placing an hourly rate on ourselves. It's going to vary from person to person, and there's no black and white answer. I promise I won't come knocking on your door with my trusty calculator asking to see your maths!

Think about what your life would look like if you could spend all your time on the high-value tasks you identified in the last section. Would you have more money? Would you be ticking off your goals at the speed of light? Would you feel happier? More accomplished? More successful?

Now think about what you would pay yourself if you could live your life like that. $100 an hour? $500 an hour? $5000 an hour? Arrive at a sum that feels good to you, and set about outsourcing as much of the low-value stuff as you can. These are the tasks that you can realistically pay someone to look after for you at less than your hourly rate.

Options to outsource

There are a wealth of options available to help you start to hand over these tasks to talented individuals, from the more 'old school' possibilities, to apps and platforms designed especially to help people like you make their lives easier.

The 'old school' option

Ads in the paper, a note in the local shop window, a friend of a friend of a friend … All of these methods are tried and tested when it comes to finding someone to give you a dig out.

Social media

I have had great success with outsourcing tasks using the connectivity that social media affords, including finding my current assistant. Putting a shout-out on our social channels is free and easy, plus finding someone from within my network is generally a safer bet for me than a total random. You're more likely to find someone with shared values, plus there's the 'insurance policy' of connections in common, so both of us are extra motivated to make the relationship work.

The other advantage to social media is that it's instant. A couple of years ago, I was falling way behind on my Christmas shopping, and I was running out of time as gifts needed to be mailed to Ireland. It was an exceptionally active time in the business, and I was despairing about how I'd get everything organised by the mailing cut-off date.

I did what I always do in times when I'm feeling overwhelmed. I wrote a list, choosing the gifts I wanted to buy for each person. I then did a Facebook shout-out asking if anyone knew anyone who could help me for a couple of days the following week.

My cousin Michael happened to have a friend travelling in Sydney who was keen to top up her holiday spending money. She came to my office, I handed her the list and my bank card, and off she went. In two days, all my shopping was done, wrapped and safely on its way to Ireland, and I felt extraordinarily proud of myself.

I think I paid her $300 altogether, which is obviously quite a heavy premium on top of the expense of buying the Christmas gifts. However, the value I got from that was far beyond $300, as it effectively bought me back two full days of time to focus on the high-value tasks at hand – namely landing some major clients and guiding the team through a hectic period when we had a lot of client campaigns moving through the business.

Outsourcing platforms

There are also a number of platforms available to help us outsource.

The first that comes to mind is Airtasker. Founded in 2012 by Timothy Fung, Airtasker enables you to upload a task with a guide price of what you'd be willing to pay someone to complete it, along with a deadline for when you need it done by.

People then make an offer to you to do the task, for the rate you suggested or a rate they choose themselves. Those who take tasks on the platform have ratings and reviews, which you can use to help guide you on who to choose for the task.

Once you have selected someone, you exchange private messages via the platform to coordinate the task. Once it's done, you release the funds and Airtasker pays the person.

The tasks range from cleaning to gardening to more specific tasks. A quick search today threw up people looking for help to move a fridge, deliver 1000 bread rolls to a local primary school, convert a two-page drug pamphlet into Chinese and square up an apartment's arches.

I have used Airtasker a lot, both for my business and personally: to transport items, have our front garden cleaned up, edit video footage and install a curtain rail. Our house was like a bombsite the day after we moved in. The floors were grubby as we had moved on a rainy day and all the movement of furniture had left dust everywhere. Our cleaner at our old house couldn't be booked at late notice, so I popped a task up on Airtasker at 8 a.m. and at 12 p.m. the best cleaner we have ever had arrived to work his magic on the house.

Operation Outsource

One of my mentees, Janine, runs a very successful and high-growth mortgage broking business, Ikaya. Facing an avalanche of new clients looking for loans (a very high-quality problem), she made 'delegate' her word for the week and set about handing over as much personal admin as she could.

Her laundry had been neglected and dry clothes were piling up in her living room. As she was working from home, the mess was really getting to her, but she couldn't devote time to it as the client deadlines needed to take priority.

Enter Airtasker! She uploaded a task onto the platform and later that day a woman arrived to spend thirty minutes sorting and folding Janine's laundry. The result was neatly stacked laundry that Janine could pop into cupboards in a couple of minutes, clearing her apartment of clutter so that she could fully focus on her work. This luxury cost Janine $20 and the woman who had done the task made some extra cash for easy work.

Other tasks that Janine outsourced that week were having her groceries unpacked, including dividing her bulk meat order from the butcher into smaller portions so she could freeze them in individual bags, and getting someone to enter her fifteen years of travel onto the online citizenship application portal (using her five passports, air tickets and a spreadsheet that Janine had prepared earlier).

Other outsourcing operations currently include Helpling (out-sourced cleaning), Zoom2U (courier service), Fiverr (outsourced creative projects) and Jarvis (personal butler at a flat hourly rate).

Guidelines for outsourcing

1. Know exactly what you want your outsourcer to do.
2. Give a clear brief – wasted time means wasted dollars (your dollars).
3. Establish a communication structure.
4. Provide clear deadlines and priorities.
5. Create a feedback loop – from them to you and you to them.
6. Be organised!

Do not feel guilty

Sure, you could beat yourself up for handing over tasks that you could quite easily do yourself. Or you could remember these three facts:

1. By outsourcing this task, you are creating an income for someone.
2. By outsourcing this task, you are investing in your own sanity – and reducing resentment both of the task itself and the people in your life.

3. By outsourcing this task, you are setting an example to others by not trying to do everything yourself.

> **The GRO list**
>
> 1. Download the high/low-value task worksheet from my website and use it to first sort through the tasks related to your business or career, and then (using a second sheet) to tackle any home-related tasks.
> 2. Ascertain what your hourly rate will be.
> 3. Estimate how much it would cost you to pay other people to do your low-value tasks.
> 4. Run your first outsourcing experiment!

CHAPTER 12

Overcoming procrastination

I recently ran a workshop on getting organised, which had twenty-five people in attendance. To kick off, I went around the group asking what their number-one challenge was when it came to getting organised. I was surprised when almost half of them said that their biggest block was procrastination – and so I decided it would be smart to include a chapter on that very topic in this book.

According to the *Oxford English Dictionary*, procrastination is 'the action of delaying or postponing something'.

Learning to overcome procrastination is one of the most important life skills we can have. It is all too easy to defer doing what we know in our hearts we should be doing at a specific moment. In fact, for many of you reading these words, procrastination is probably the biggest block getting in the way of where you're at now and the life you truly want to be living.

Tony Robbins was once asked about the biggest change he had made in his life to go from being broke, overweight and single to the person he is today (i.e. loaded, healthy and happily married). His answer hit me hard. It was, he said, a sense of urgency. Going about our lives with a sense of urgency, we grip up each task on our list with zeal, and work effectively on it until it's done.

The polar opposite is a life of chronic procrastination, where we should-a, would-a, could-a ourselves with delays, keeping ourselves from getting to the work that, really, would see us owning our goals. In fact, I can think of no sneakier way that we cheat ourselves out of success than putting off working on tasks that would move us forward. It's the ultimate act of self-sabotage.

In the book *Flow*, Mihaly Csikszentmihalyi compares pleasure with enjoyment. Pleasure, he explains, is a short-term win that we derive from activities like eating delicious food, watching TV or having a massage. Enjoyment, however, comes from working on tasks that are productive and get us closer to our goals.

The mistake many of us make is that we pursue pleasure day to day, rather than the ultimately more fulfilling activity of enjoyment. For example, we'll prioritise checking our Instagram feed (pleasure) over updating our résumé so we can apply for our dream job (enjoyment).

Procrastination also wastes time. I hate waste generally – I'm that person who'll finish a gigantic meal just so the food doesn't go to waste. However, my biggest bugbear is wasting time. As the designer Tom Ford said, 'Time and silence are the most luxurious things today.'

I value my time highly and I cannot cope with it being wasted. This is why I get even more irritated with myself when I catch myself procrastinating about something – I am hyper-aware that I'm wasting my own time, and no one else's, when I fill hours with doing anything other than the task I'm supposed to be doing. There's good reason for the phrase 'Procrastination is the thief of time'.

Another major problem that procrastination brings with it is how it feeds our negative self-talk loop. We delay getting started on a task; we then cop some kind of shit for that delay (from a client, family member or ourselves); we tell ourselves we're useless at being organised; then, when the next task rolls around, we tell ourselves we're even more useless, we procrastinate even longer, cop more shit, and so on ...

When we succeed at dodging procrastination and tackling a task head on, we feel hyper-organised, on our game and like we're generally winning at life – and we tell ourselves that. The next task pops up and we bulldoze through it, as we're buoyed by our previous success.

I am going to change teams for a moment and say that our friend procrastination does serve us well sometimes. I'm sure, like me, you've had experience of delaying starting something, only to find out that if you had done it when you were supposed to, you'd be in a worse-off situation.

A few years ago, I was all set to send a letter of offer to a new hire after a very positive second interview. For some reason, I put off writing and sending the letter to her first thing the next morning as planned. That window gave a friend who had previously worked with the hire to come back to me with some rather unflattering feedback on the person. As you can imagine, I was pretty happy that I had procrastinated on this occasion!

Sometimes it also forces us to ask some hard questions, which perhaps we might not have asked had we started on the task at hand immediately. During our procrastination 'process', we might ask ourselves how important this task really is, consider easier or better ways to complete it, or decide not to do it at all.

We all have times when procrastinating saves us from ourselves; however, I would warrant that those instances are few and far between, so we'll be focusing this chapter on doing *less* procrastinating rather than *more*!

A note on willpower

Before we begin, we should give a hat tip to our friend Mr Will Power. This is the number-one resource we need to draw on in our battle against our foe Procrastination, and it will be required regardless of the reason we're procrastinating.

Like anyone, Mr Will Power gets better the more he practises. It comes back to our neural muscle – the more we work it, the stronger it gets. In her book *The Willpower Project*, psychologist Kelly McGonigal discusses the three forces of willpower:

1. I won't – this is essentially our ability to resist temptation, saying no even when every fibre of our being wants to say 'yes'. That might be saying no to one more episode of *The Good Wife* before bed or that triple chocolate brownie when we've just quit sugar.

2. I will – this one helps us accomplish tasks that are unpleasant, yet are necessary for us to achieve goals – for example, updating that résumé so we can apply for a new job, or getting up at 4 a.m. to train for a half-marathon.
3. I want – this power helps us remember what we really want from our lives, and in doing so keeps us on track by guiding our actions day to day.

In defeating procrastination, we need to draw on each of these powers – and sometimes we need all three.

Why we procrastinate

There is no one reason why we procrastinate. In order to look at the issue from a few different angles, I have identified four key reasons why we delay on starting critical tasks, and made some suggestions for each to help you out of your procrastination rut.

> The first step to overcoming procrastination is to identify exactly *why* it is we're deferring a particular task.

There are umpteen reasons, motivations or explanations for why we procrastinate about a task; however, for the purposes of this book, I'm going to boil them down into four distinct camps:

1. *We don't want to do it* – it's boring, hard or pointless.
2. *We don't know how to do it* – it's our first time undertaking this task, or we're just not that confident about doing it.

3. *We're scared of the task* – it involves a difficult conversation, or getting uncomfortable in some other way.
4. *We don't know where to start* – we're intimidated by the task's 'bigness'.

We're going to unpack each of these individually, and I'll make some suggestions as to how we go about tackling them.

1. You don't want to do it
Do you actually have to do it?
The first thing I ask myself when there's a task that's been sitting on my to-do list for a few days is: do I actually *need* to do it? Very often we add tasks to our lists that, in fact, are not going to get us closer to our overall goals. It is extremely frustrating to spend hours on a task that – really – we don't see the point in doing.

If you're in this boat, then consider what would happen if you didn't do this task. What would the impact be? If you can live with whatever that looks like, then perhaps you don't need to complete the task at all, and you can move on to something that will actually serve you and those around you.

Have a clear space
The 'I don't want to do it' reason for procrastinating is the most perilous for pre-task tidying/organising. When I needed to study for an exam at school, I could spend hours tidying my bedroom as a means of procrastinating instead of just opening my books and getting started. Doing a quick tidy of our workspace prevents us from falling into that particular trap.

Set up the day before

Having your computer set up, any relevant documents to hand and collating any other information you'll require to complete the task the day before you actually do it gives a great headstart to getting it done.

For example, I was recently procrastinating on filing a few claims on our pet insurance – this kind of mindless admin drives me nuts, between registering for online access and scanning receipts ... I get itchy about it.

I put it on my to-do list for the following day, pulled out the policy document and receipts, and left them on my desk before I finished up for the day. The next morning, I felt like I had already started the task and I got cracking as soon as I got to 'pet insurance claim' on my list.

Confuse your brain

So you've decided that you do, in fact, need to do this task. What now?

When we're doing something we enjoy doing, we get a hit of dopamine – the neurotransmitter that governs our brain's reward and pleasure centres. Getting a tonne of likes on a social media post fires up our dopamine (hence the prevalence of social media addiction!), as does sipping an ice-cold beer or spending time with those we love. As you can imagine, when we're doing something we don't enjoy – like a boring task we've been delaying starting – we have the opposite response.

After Wade and I had moved into our first home with just the two of us, we embarked on a mission to blend our finances. This turned out to be a much more complicated process than I expected.

As Wade was a financial adviser at the time, he insisted that we do it properly. This meant we needed to get our insurances sorted, close down defunct bank accounts that each of us had, open up some new ones and automate how our salaries got distributed between accounts each month. We had regular 'meetings' to work through it all, which would go on forever (okay, I'm exaggerating ... a couple of hours).

As I've already shared, this kind of admin gives me the shits. It didn't help that I was used to flying solo with money, and having to take into account someone else's financial set-up, and negotiate each step of our new system, made the task a lot more laborious. I found the whole thing insanely boring, not to mention *deeply* unromantic.

I came to dread these meetings, as I'm sure Wade did, too. Around this time I was working with a coach who suggested cancelling out the negative association I had with these sessions by aligning them with more enjoyable occasions. She suggested opening a bottle of nice wine while we talked money, which would soften the boring finance talk and make it marginally more enjoyable.

When I'm really struggling to get in the zone on something that I'm fully expecting not to enjoy doing, I'll kick some dopamine into play to trick my brain into thinking it is, in fact, having a blast. A few pieces of dark chocolate is a surefire way for me to get some dopamine cranking, which gives me enough motivation to get whatever the task is underway. And as I'm sure you've experienced, getting started is the hardest bit by far.

Think about what makes you happy, and try to match that up with getting started on a tough task. It might be sipping on some red wine, playing your favourite band on high volume or watching a funny YouTube video before you get started (just make sure you stop at one!).

Self-incentivise

As you'll know from our chat about habits, I am a huge fan of self-incentivising. Setting myself little rewards works a treat for me, particularly when there's something uninspiring on my list. Chocolate, a hot drink, a walk – knowing I have something nice to look forward to once the task is completed gives me a little extra fuel to get it done.

2. You don't know how to do it

When I've got something on my list that I've never done before, it's likely that I'll procrastinate for a few days about getting it done – or even weeks if it's something really big. It was only when reading Neil Fiore's *The Now Habit* that I realised why I do this.

It's born from a fear of failure. He describes procrastination as a strategy to avoid the fear of failure. So if I delay starting something, then I haven't really tried, therefore I haven't failed …

Get clear on what you need to do

First, though, do you have a clear idea of what it is you need to do?

I asked one of my team to do something recently, and immediately forgot all about it despite having a record of being scarily efficient. It was only when the person I had asked him to deal with followed up again via email that I realised he hadn't carried out the task.

When I addressed it with him, we explored why he had dropped the ball and we realised that I hadn't given him clear instructions on how to go about the task. As a result, he was confused about what he actually needed to do and consequently procrastinated on doing it for an entire week – which was totally unlike him. Once we had spent a few minutes talking through it, he went away and knocked it over immediately.

> Taking some time out to get a clear idea of what is expected from the task can often nip any procrastination in the bud, and increase your chances of getting it done well.

See the task as a work in progress

For four and a half years, my business The Remarkables Group had represented influencers and essentially brokered deals with brands on their behalf. I made a pretty momentous decision to completely change the business model late last year – as I believed we could serve brands better as an independent influencer strategy house, rather than a talent agent.

Much of my time in the immediate days and weeks following this decision was spent seeing the influencers we represented to communicate the change, helping some transition to new management, steadying the ship with the team and managing the industry relations around the announcement.

Something I hadn't actually done was mapped out exactly what this new business model would look like, beyond a one-page brain dump of thoughts. It was pretty silly in retrospect, given that by wrapping up our previous business model we were kissing goodbye to $2 million of annual revenue!

I set up some meetings with brands to present our new model, and procrastinated for three weeks on sitting down and writing the presentation that would showcase it. Every single day I wrote 'new model presentation' on the MITs of my to-do list, and then shamelessly skipped ahead to other, easier tasks. Every day for three weeks!

I was livid with myself for procrastinating on such a vital task. After all, without this presentation I wouldn't be able to sell the new model to clients. That would mean sweet fuck-all revenue, which would mean letting my team go, closing the business and me updating my résumé for the first time in seven years. Even going through this worst-case scenario didn't prompt me into action!

The block – a pretty big one – was that I had no idea what this new model should look like. I didn't know how to structure the strategic process, what the revenue model should be, how the team allocation would work ... nothing! I was afraid that if I did it, it would be wrong, and that I would have failed at the first hurdle after this massive leap of faith I had taken.

Then I realised a couple of important things:

1. There was no way this could be 'wrong', as it had never been done before. The model we were designing was a first to market; therefore, there simply wasn't a right way or wrong way to do it. I needed to remove the idea of getting it to what it *should* be and simply create what I thought it *could* be.
2. I was trying to avoid the new model failing by not putting pen to paper on what it would look like, when in truth I was failing myself – and my team – by not getting started on it at all!

I made a deal with myself that the new model was a work in progress and, in fact, it always would be. The first step was to design a business that would address the biggest problems our clients were experiencing right now, and we could evolve the model as and when we needed to do so beyond that. If there were parts of the new model that didn't work, then we could adapt the model to resolve those parts.

This new mindset gave me no small sense of relief, and I felt I had permission to get started – finally! – on the presentation.

Skill up

If the task you're procrastinating on *has* been done before, hooray – you're in luck! This means that by spending a small amount of time skilling yourself up, you can give yourself a headstart to getting underway.

Is there someone you can ask for some pointers? Is there a YouTube video tutorial you can watch? Is there a book that can give you some tips?

> By arming ourselves with even a bit more information, we immediately increase our odds of not just getting started on the task at hand, but aceing it in the process.

3. You're scared of the task

We all have stuff that scares the crap out of us, that makes us deeply uncomfortable. For me, having difficult conversations ranks pretty highly up there. It might be ending a business relationship, giving feedback to one of my team or resolving a conflict with a family member.

If you're anything like I used to be, you'll circle for days around dealing with that unsavoury task – with the usual result that the original issue is ten times worse by the time you actually deal with it. Or worse – you don't deal with it and it saps your happiness for months on end.

I've worked hard on this one, and as a result I don't find conflict anywhere near as scary as I used to.

When I'm procrastinating on a scary task, there are a few things I try to remind myself of.

Remember it's never as bad as you think it's going to be

As you can imagine, going to see each of our talent when I made the decision to change the business model was terrifying. Some of them we had represented for years and telling them that we were no longer going to be able to do that had me awake for several nights. Without exception, the twenty-three conversations went better than I could even have hoped and my endless worrying was unfounded.

Focus on the energy you'll free up

A few months ago, one of my mentees came to the realisation that she needed to let one of her team members go. The person was operating far below the capacity that she should have been at, had a pretty average attitude and my mentee couldn't see a role for her long-term in her business. This situation occupied much of our sessions for two months, and she procrastinated on having the conversation with the person. She had a deep-seated dread of difficult conversations. As you can imagine, it weighed heavily on her mind and distracted her from focusing on other parts of her business – most especially growing revenue.

When the conversation had *finally* been had, I could feel my mentee's relief in her text message, sent from the other side of the country! By our next monthly session, she had gripped up her sales pipeline, hired a new team member and was immeasurably more upbeat.

While I was happy that she and her business were in a better place, I did wonder about the lost productivity that resulted from the two months of gearing up to deal with the situation.

> When you have a difficult task ahead, focus on the energy you'll free up once you're out the other side of it. It helps enormously to avoid the procrastination trap.

4. You don't know where to start

We've all had tasks that seem so ginormous that we literally do not know where, or how, to start on them. They feel like insurmountable mountains in our way and we spend days – or weeks – trying to motivate ourselves to get them underway.

The amount of resistance we feel correlates with the scale of the task

In Steven Pressfield's book *Do the Work*, he introduces the concept of 'resistance' – our natural push-back when some work needs to get done. The bigger the task, the more resistance to it we feel.

We might have a small amount of resistance to sending an email to a client, but it's relatively easy to overcome. Writing a full client strategy from scratch, though, is a different story –

our resistance is very high, which results in us procrastinating for longer.

> Remembering that it's completely normal to feel the dead weight of resistance when we're facing an intimidatingly large job helps us to work through it.

Break the task up into chunks

My team is probably sick of me reciting: 'How do you eat an elephant? One bite at a time.'

Chunking large tasks down into bite-size pieces makes the task itself a lot more approachable.

When I have something big on my list, the first thing I'll do is look at the overall outcome and work back from that with small, manageable steps.

This book is a perfect example. Rather than just putting 'write book' on my to-do list for weeks on end, instead I mapped it out chapter by chapter. Then I filled out each chapter heading with bullets of the key points I would include in each chapter. When it came time to start writing, I would put the specific chapter for that day on my to-do list (pre-baby!) and now the sections within each chapter (post-baby!).

Another instance is when I got started on the presentation of our new business model. Writing 'do new model presentation' on my to-do list was too daunting, so instead I took a week-long approach.

For Day 1, I resolved to start the PowerPoint presentation and put titles on the slides. On Day 2, I filled in bullet points on each slide. On Day 3, I highlighted gaps where I would need the team's input and briefed them. On Day 4, I created the charts I wanted to include and sourced images. On Day 5, I filled in the gaps around the bullet points and plugged in the team's contributions. Then it was done!

Giving ourselves the opportunity to tick off smaller goals not only helps us get the job done, it also gives us more of a sense of accomplishment as we work through it. Completing the various steps of the presentation each day gave me a solid feeling of achievement, rather than plugging away at one big daunting goal day after day.

Work on it for a small period of time

I remember trainer Michelle Bridges sharing her number-one tip to get motivated to exercise: tell yourself you'll train for just twenty minutes. If you want to finish after that, you can. Of course, by the time we're exercising for that long, we're actually not minding it too much – in fact, we might even be enjoying ourselves!

For me, often the hardest part of exercising is just starting, and the logistics involved to get to that point. Those steps include downing tools by a specific time, changing into my exercise gear and getting to the yoga studio in time for my class. Once I'm on the mat, it feels like plain sailing from there on.

I apply this method to getting started on a big task – promising myself I'll do it for just twenty minutes, and I can stop then. Nine times out of ten, I've found flow by that point and I keep going.

This insight is what makes the Pomodoro Technique so effective. Created by Francesco Cirillo while he was at university, it's a super-easy approach to aid productivity – and nix procrastination.

Cirillo used a basic tomato (*pomodoro*) shaped timer and set it for twenty-five minutes. He then committed to working with full focus for that twenty-five minutes – no more and no less. Once the alarm sounded, he took a five-minute break before returning to work by setting the timer for another block of twenty-five minutes. And so on.

The beauty of this approach is that it breaks the entire day down into chunks of twenty-five productive minutes. The trick to mastering the Pomodoro Technique is correctly estimating how many Pomodoro sessions a particular task will take – which comes with practice. I don't use the technique myself, but Wade adopted it years ago when I mentioned it to him and he has used it religiously since.

If procrastination is an ongoing challenge for you, try working with the Pomodoro Technique for a week and see whether it helps.

Create cues

We spoke in Chapter 5 about how the first step of a habit is the cue. For smokers, their morning coffee might trigger the action to smoke. For me, turning the lights down at night is my cue to my body to start preparing for sleep.

It is possible to create cues for ourselves that, when used regularly, help to prevent us from procrastinating and enter into a productive flow state more quickly.

Author and speaker Danielle Laporte wears a certain beanie while she's writing a book. For many of us, a strong coffee probably gets us in the zone – AKA 'procaffeinating'! We've already learned how entrepreneur Peter Moriarty plays certain music in the morning to rev himself up for the day ahead and different music in the evening to wind down.

Scent is a great cue for me. I'm sure you've experienced the power of scent to transport you to a specific time or place, or remind you of a certain person. It might be a shampoo you used on a foreign holiday, a certain kind of food cooking or the perfume of a loved one. I have used certain essential oils and candles for years to help me get in the zone. In fact, I've just created my own 'Get Shit Done' essential oil blend with spa brand Ikou. Writing this book was the perfect project to test out different blends!

Where we work is also key. I often suggest to my mentees who are struggling to find/make the time for working 'on' their businesses rather than 'in' them to work somewhere different from their usual office for their strategy time – a regular library, café or other area. This doesn't just insulate them from the usual office distractions; it also gives them a physical space that cues them to being in the strategy zone rather than their everyday zone.

The GRO list

1. Identify three tasks about which you have procrastinated – or are still procrastinating – in recent weeks.
2. Choose which of the four main reasons for procrastinating applies to each of these instances, remembering that there may be more than one reason.
3. Using the techniques I have suggested, design a 'recipe' that would help you avoid procrastinating on this task or a similar task in future.

CHAPTER 13

Family

When I have spoken professionally about the topic of 'Getting Seriously F*cking Organised' (the chapter title in my first book) and we get to the Q&A part of my talk, the same question is always asked. It comes from someone in the audience who is a parent, and it generally goes like this: 'This is all really great, but how do you do this *with kids*?'

And it's a fair enough question. After all, here I was talking on stage having only had to get myself out the door that morning. I couldn't even imagine trying to wrangle a couple of small people from the point where they woke up to getting them to their daycare/kindergarten/school washed, dressed, fed and loved!

Wade and I travelled to Queenstown a few years ago for the wedding of friends, and over a perfectly Kiwi dinner of lamb and pinot noir, we were discussing morning routines. As I listed the various steps of my leisurely, time-abundant morning start (as it was then), one of our friends quite literally snorted her wine through her nose. She was the mum of two kids and our morning routines probably could not have been more different.

So if you were reading the morning routine chapter wondering how the hell you would squeeze all of that in with your tribe, I hear you. That's why I felt it was important to devote a chapter in this book to figuring out this organised gig with the consideration of the family commitments that many of us have.

As I write this chapter, our eight-week-old girl Lexi is having her morning nap in the next room. I am a newly minted member of the Parents' Club, and therefore I'm in absolutely no position to call myself an expert in this area.

Over the last few weeks, Wade and I have realised very quickly that we are most certainly not in the driving seat anymore. Everything now is in her two very tiny hands – when we sleep, when we eat, when we work. For two people who relish their freedom and measure themselves by their achievements and efficiency each day, this has been *quite* the wake-up call!

I see many people around me who are managing to run a business (or several businesses), keep themselves healthy and stay sane while also doing a stellar job of parenting their kids – and some of them are parenting solo.

As a big believer in modelling the behaviour of others, I looked to them to study how they do it. This involved observing these people closely and asking tonnes of questions. The insights and common themes I noticed form the basis of this chapter.

The reason, not the excuse

Before we begin, I want to share something that has helped me as I prepared to step into this new role.

When Wade and I were having The Conversation to decide to start trying for a baby, we each shared the fears we had about the next life phase we were hopefully about to embark upon. We had both always wanted children, but now the decision was being made and it made the whole concept very real and not a little scary.

I realised that I had a tonne of fears around having a family, one of the biggest being how I would continue to run my business.

I told Wade that I would need to downscale our business goals and curb our global ambitions for a few years. I simply couldn't envision how I could manage to go full tilt, as I was used to doing, with a baby on the way and definitely not once they arrived.

Wade told me that we needed to: *make them the reason, not the excuse.*

This would be key to us having the lives that we individually wanted, but also be the best role models we could for our children. Take moving to a new country as an example. If we made our kids the reason for that, we could say that they would have new experiences they wouldn't otherwise have had, they would have two parents who were setting a benchmark for how to achieve their dreams, and we would have fun as a family.

The opposing mindset to this would be that it's too difficult to move countries with a family, therefore it's better to stay in Sydney and limit our ambitions to Australia alone.

Early in our pregnancy, I was just starting to acknowledge my feelings about the business not being the right model and was trying to figure out what to do about it. I knew I needed to make a change, and that that change would be a defining moment not just for the business but for my future life combining a real-life baby with my 'first-born' (The Remarkables Group).

I had two avenues available to me. The first saw me staying true to the big aspirations I had when I started the business – such as a global offer, a growing team and ambitious revenue targets. The second saw me winding down the business and instead becoming a one-woman consultancy, accepting short-term contracts that I would fit around the baby.

Avenue 1 scared the crap out of me, and considering it with a baby in the mix made my head spin. Avenue 2 felt tempting. It was a safe option, I wouldn't need to stretch myself and I would likely make a lot more money in the short-term.

Wade reminded me again of our commitment to make a family the reason, not the excuse. I saw immediately that going with Avenue 2 would be me using a baby as an excuse to play small – something that, while insanely appealing during tough times, I had never seriously considered doing.

When it comes to our journey to getting remarkably organised, try to make your family the reason for you committing to this, rather than an excuse not to try. We've already talked at length about the benefits of getting into the driving seat of our lives. We're calmer, more efficient and happier. When we manage to operate from this state, how good a role model are we being, not only for our kids, but also everyone around us?

When you master the organisation of your life, you'll have more time, energy and headspace to devote to your family – and I'm fairly sure they won't have a problem with that!

Enlist as much help as you can

One of the strongest themes I noticed with those successful parents who I studied was their proactive nature in seeking help with the juggling act that having a family entails.

If we look at families fifty years ago, it was unlikely that the mother was working and so she spent all of her time taking care of the children, looking after the house and picking up all the life admin. This meant that the father could work as many hours as he needed to, knowing that the kids were being looked after and that life minutiae was being tended to.

Today it's likely that both parents are working, meaning that all the child rearing and life 'stuff' is being allocated across two people – or, more likely, the mother is still shouldering the lion's share of it.

Most men today are very involved with their homes and children; however, I've observed (and experienced first hand) that, for whatever reason, we women tend to take on more of the 'mental' load – thinking, planning, organising, remembering ... It can all be rather exhausting at times.

I'm sure I'm not alone in sometimes wishing that I had a wife myself to remember the countless little things that need to be bought, collected or done every single day. In fact, the very clever and funny Annabel Crabb wrote a book on this topic. *The Wife Drought* makes for eye-opening reading.

As the vast majority of us won't have the incredible help that a full-time 'wife' would offer, it becomes necessary to outsource elements of our home and family life to keep the whole machine rumbling along. This is the number-one common trait I see in those who are simultaneously having consistent success on both the business/career and family fronts.

One woman for whom I have enormous respect – and want to be like when I grow up! – is Emma Isaacs, Global CEO of Business Chicks. I've been fortunate to have some quality chats with Emma on my various adventures with her business; from the red earth of Australia's Uluru to the turquoise waters of Necker Island.

As you can imagine, with my future family plans I took every opportunity I could to learn about the behind-the-scenes of running a global (and enormously successful) business, and being a kickass mum to five little people.

Emma makes it abundantly clear that she is not flying solo on this mission, and that there is in fact a small army of people in her support team who enable her to do what she does. This army includes her husband Rowan, her mum, nannies, cleaners and housekeepers. In fact, a factor in her and Rowan's decision to relocate their brood from Sydney to LA was that the cost of childcare and home help in the United States was approximately half what they were paying in Australia.

We were on a tour of Uluru a few years ago and Emma had baby Ryder strapped to her in a baby carrier. Someone in the group commented that Ryder was wearing a lot of star-patterned clothes over the three days we were in the desert. Emma replied that she had no idea what was in his bag, nor did she care. The nanny had packed it and, as that was one less task Emma herself had to do, she was happy.

You may not be in a position to have a team of help on an ongoing basis, so perhaps a more casual option would help you. My friend Julie Masters has a one-year-old daughter and is one of the smartest business people I know. She and her husband both have their own businesses, and they have a very clever on/off approach to childcare.

When she had their little girl, Julie sent a message to all the parents she knew asking for the names and numbers of the nannies and babysitters they knew and trusted. She entered each name into her phone after 'Nanny', so 'Nanny Kate', 'Nanny Sarah', etc. When she needs a babysitter, she sends a group text to all the nannies in her phone (six in total) specifying when she needs someone, and books whoever comes back to her first.

Having non-family members care for your children may not be for you, or it may not be available to you for whatever reason. If this is the case, then consider what other responsibilities you can hand over. It might be house cleaning (you already know I'm a big fan of outsourcing that particular task!) or ordering groceries online. You might like to use my Time Task Audit worksheet from my website to help you identify which tasks you could potentially hand over.

Create systems

Systems and processes get talked about *a lot* in entrepreneurial circles. Systems are any repeatable processes in a business that can theoretically take place without the leader's direct action.

A system is a method of doing something that can be done the same way, over and over, as efficiently as possible. Some of the benefits of embedding systems in a business are the increased ability to scale, consistency of work and reduced costs as the team is working more efficiently.

The idea is to build systems for the everyday things that get done in a business, thereby reducing the instance of mistakes and freeing up time and energy to devote to cracking the bigger challenges.

I find it fascinating that we rarely – if ever – talk about the importance of systems in our homes. For me, there are little things that Wade and I have built into our daily tasks at home that make life that tiny bit easier by removing irritating stones in our shoes. I'll give you three examples:

1. The dishwasher taking ages to empty

A rudimentary system we follow is putting all the forks in one section of the cutlery holder in the dishwasher, the knives in another, random lids and appliance attachments in another, and so on. This means that when it comes time to empty the dishwasher, we can chuck all the spoons in their spot in the drawer in one go. Not having to sort through each item of cutlery one by one as we empty it means we shave a good five minutes off the chore.

2. Wade forgetting to hang out laundry

I seem to have a tab in my brain that reminds me that a load of laundry is finished, and therefore needs to be hung out. Wade does not have this tab, and will often forget he's put laundry on until I discover it when I'm about to put on another load three days later. At this point, the 'clean' clothes are musty and need to be washed again, and I go nuts. Now if we put a load of washing on, we leave the folding door of the laundry open – this is the signal for Wade that he needs to hang clothes out to dry.

3. Coming down to a messy living room

Since we had our little girl, we seem to spend a hell of a lot more time at home, and the sofa plays host to most of our evenings. Coming downstairs to a messy living room the next morning with a hungry baby, hungry me and the inevitable newborn laundry to face was a big morale killer.

A pretty organic system was started, which simply meant we tidied the living room before hauling our tired asses up to bed at night. This involved folding away the various blankets we had used, straightening the throw on the sofa, plumping the cushions, bringing rubbish and cups or glasses to the kitchen, and packing away our laptops if we had been using them. Now coming downstairs is much more pleasant every morning and we feel we're starting the day with clear space, and clearer minds.

Let's be honest. None of this is remotely glamorous or cool. However, these small systems save time, stress and headspace every single day in our home. As we adapt to life with our little girl, we're creating more systems to ease the workload that her presence brings with it.

Another common thread among those with whom I spoke for this chapter was their creation of systems for their homes and families. Like us, they have come to rely on these systems as small anchors in the daily chaos and unpredictability that having a family involves. Many of these systems are born out of a stressful episode.

Take my friend Julie as an example. She and her husband Josh split their days to look after their daughter, Tali, and they also have a handful of nannies who take care of her. Julie said each of them could lose an hour trying to get out of the house as they packed the change bag – trying to keep an eye on Tali while running upstairs to get a hat, downstairs to get sunscreen, and so on.

A simple system was born where there was a checklist of all the elements that were required in the change bag, and it was the job of whoever had it last to restock it. That meant if Josh took Tali to the playground, it fell to him to ensure that there were adequate nappies, changes of clothes, etc. in the bag so that the person taking her next time could confidently grab the bag and step out of the house as quickly as Tali would allow them to.

I realised the value of their system myself just a couple of days ago, when I went to tackle a poo explosion with Lexi in a five-star hotel, only to realise that there were no nappies in the change bag.

This involved closing up the dirty nappy, dressing her again, hauling our bags out of the bathroom and walking back across the hotel where Wade, thankfully, was waiting and was able to go out and track down nappies. A failed first stop at the pharmacy and a successful second stop at a convenience store later, and we managed to do the nappy change. The result of this lapse was twenty minutes of time lost, unnecessary stress and poor Lexi sitting in a filthy nappy for longer than she needed to. Guess what we do now? Yep, we have a change bag system!

Identifying opportunities to create systems in your family and home is an extremely worthwhile exercise, and it's also one that can involve the whole family.

A consummate expert in this area is blogger Katrina Springer, AKA The Organised Housewife. She has tried and tested many systems herself, which she then shares with her hundreds of thousands of followers.

Some of the examples of systems she shares on her website specifically for families are:

- labelling boxes with the type of toys to help kids clean up themselves
- having a small shelving unit per child next to the front door to keep all school requirements organised (e.g. bottom drawer: school shoes, middle drawer: homework and school diary, etc.)
- colour-coding family towels so everyone knows which towel belongs to who.

One of my friends, Melanie Baker, has provided her son with a whiteboard that has his morning activities written on it, which helps him to get himself organised in the morning. The whiteboard includes making his bed, brushing his teeth, getting dressed, eating breakfast – and Thomas ticks off each activity as he does it during the morning.

Routine to the max

We have already covered the topic of routine in detail in earlier chapters, and I would warrant that if you have kids you have discovered the power of routine already.

The benefits for us adults of having positive routines embedded into our lives are increased productivity, feeling calmer and having more headspace to enjoy our days. For kids, it gives them a sense of security and the resulting feeling of calmness. As Emmy Samtani says: 'The kids really respond well to the predictability of having a ritual.'

According to website Kidspot, some of the reasons why kids thrive on routine include:

1. helping them to understand time and time management
2. getting them used to having chores
3. establishing important habits such as brushing teeth and hair
4. strengthening relationships by focusing on time together as a family.

A recent Education.com article explained that because little ones don't fully understand how time works, they don't order their lives in terms of hours and minutes. Instead they order them by the events that take place. When events take place in the same sequence every day, children have a better grasp of their world and feel more secure. Therefore, a predictable routine helps them organise their lives. When they know what to expect, they have more confidence in not just themselves, but the world around them.[1]

Of the parents I grilled for this chapter, it was clear that having a firmly embedded routine for their kids – but also for themselves – was a fundamental reason why they could do what they do. Nosey as I am, I asked them to describe their routines in detail for your reading pleasure ...

Jules Lund's morning routine

'6 a.m. wake-up. Set the house up for my wife and two daughters to wake up to with cruisy music, gas fireplace and, if I'm really good, a cup of tea for my wife. Although often she makes me one. I'll cook up omelettes I've made the night before. Hit 10 minutes of Smiling Mind meditation, before doing an hour of emails – mostly responding to actions needed from our UK office who've been busy while we sleep. Pack a bag for after my gym session so I can shower and go straight to work.'

Sarah Pearce's morning routine

'New life as a working mother – baby comes first, so routine is attending to baby and her morning routine first. If I'm lucky and wake up before her, a quick email check or cup of tea. Otherwise, once I've taken care of her, it's now a rushed tea and toast before getting ready to get into the office. I used to have a leisurely hour for brekky and getting ready, but now with a little one – it's a mad rush and little effort to get dressed and into the office!'

Kelly Exeter's morning routine

'4.15 a.m. wake up, 4.15–4.45 a.m. drink two big glasses of water while scrolling through Instagram and Facebook, 4.45–5 a.m. check emails (clear out the crap, take note of what will require my attention later in the day), 5–6 a.m. write, 6–6.45 a.m. exercise, 7–7.30 a.m. kids' breakfast, green smoothie for myself and husband, husband gets the four-year-old out the door, 7.30–8 a.m. get myself ready for the day, 8–8.30 a.m. household chores, 8.30 a.m. take eight-year-old to school.'

Sally Obermeder's evening routine

'Get Annabelle in the shower while I make her dinner. Once she is out and eating dinner, I give Elyssa dinner, then a bath. Then Elyssa goes to bed and I make dinner for Marcus and myself. Then we eat together while Annabelle eats her dessert and we talk about our day and either watch TV with her or play games until her bedtime. After she goes to bed, I do work while Marcus goes for a walk then when he gets back we wind down together.'

Sabri Suby's evening routine

'Play with my daughter. Dinner. No phone past 6 p.m. Reading. In bed at 9 p.m.'

Emmy Samtani's evening routine

'Our evenings start from 5–5.30 p.m., this is when our "night routine" starts. It is always a very nice time in the house as the lights go down and we follow the same routine each night for my toddler: dinner, bath, quiet play, glass of milk, brush teeth, story and bed. In amongst this we manage to do the baby's night routine with feed/bath/feed and then bed once the toddler has gone down. Once all kids go down, it is shower, dinner and more work for mumma.'

When thinking about how you can establish a new routine for your family, or fine-tune the existing routines, refer back to Chapter 5.

Remember the three key factors in creating productive routines:

1. Layer them gradually, rather than biting off too much initially.
2. Remember that every family's routine is going to be different.
3. Give gold stars – reward yourself and the family when the routine is implemented successfully.

Create a communication structure

When I look at successful businesses and how they run, communication between team members is critical.

Effective communication ensures that everyone is working towards the same goal and minor issues can be ironed out before they turn into major issues. Communication is essentially another system. With our business, for example, there is a steady rhythm of meetings – covering management, operations, strategy, finance, team one-on-ones and compulsory fun (team lunches and outings).

I strive to have a relationship like my friends Richenda and Kyle Vermeulen, and love getting the download of how they run their lives whenever I see them – even more so now that I'm a mum as they are parents to a wonderful toddler themselves.

Richenda owns a fast-growing digital agency in Melbourne and manages to operate as CEO (and a bloody effective one at that) within her 32-hour work week. Her support team includes Kyle, family members and daycare.

She shared with me recently that the juggle had felt overwhelming in recent months, most especially the mental load that I know and love myself (not). Something that was helping enormously was a session every Sunday evening where she and Kyle looked at the week ahead, and allocated who was doing what: from grocery shopping to daycare pick-ups. The clarity it gave them both was amazing, she said, and it had eased a lot of the daily stress that had been building up.

My clever friend Melanie has a schedule on the fridge so that she and her husband can tell at a glance who has the kids on particular days, and they have a quick chat over dinner each evening about the plan for the next day.

My and Wade's communication has gone through phases of being structured versus unstructured over the years that we've been together. Since our daughter arrived, the importance of having a communication structure has been overwhelmingly pronounced. We can't wing it like we used to when it was just the two of us bumbling along – now we've got to (try to) be grown-ups so that she constantly has care, and so that we can each get the shit we need to get done, done.

This involves a weekly family meeting (Wade and I do most of the talking right now ...), where we each pull up our calendars for the week ahead and walk each other through what's happening for the next seven days. Right now I depend on Wade to look after Lexi if I want to go out for dinner or if I have an appointment I can't take her with me to. We'll also go through the various household tasks that need to be done and allocate a list to each of us. Getting this opportunity to plan is one of the few things I've found that helps ease the 'mental load' that I carry – once something is delegated to Wade, it comes off my ever-evolving list.

Then each evening during the week, we have a quick check-in on what's happening the next day. This has been a godsend, as we are both so used to accepting commitments without a second thought; now we need to remember that the other one has to be on hand for Baby if we're going to be on that Skype call or at that event that just dropped in.

It also saves us from falling into the trap of assumptions. Several times, I just assumed that Wade could take Lexi while I went off to do X activity the next day – I figured that he would have told me if he had something on, right?

Um, no. There is no reason that he would feel the need to inform me that he had a key meeting at 10 a.m. on Tuesday, as he assumed that I had nothing on as well!

Proactively looking at the short-term window of the next twenty-four hours means that we can catch any last-minute edits to our schedules, and it keeps the wolf of assumption from the door.

> Having some kind of communication structure will save you a hell of a lot of stress, time and resentment.

If you don't have a partner, then effective, proactive communication with your support team is still just as important – be that family members, childcare or friends. This doesn't need to be a formal weekly meeting; it could be as easy as a WhatsApp group in which people can share updates on a day-to-day basis. Wade and I now have a WhatsApp group with our nanny called 'Team Lexi' and all nanny arrangements get exchanged there so all three of us know what's happening.

Build in fudge factor

From my limited experience so far, our daughter is the most terrifyingly *moving* moving part that I have ever encountered.

Gone is the era of planning our days in minute detail, as we have had to surrender to her and what her needs, wants and wishes are from day to day. In fact, I jokingly ask *her* what the schedule for the day ahead is each morning as she has a much better idea than I do!

I learned this the hard way when she chalked up a few lengthy morning naps for a solid week. 'Aha!' I told myself, 'this is her *routine*.' I reconfigured my writing schedule for this book in line with me having a chunk of four hours every morning to focus on writing. Of course, two days later she decided not to sleep at all for an entire day – and I got no writing done whatsoever.

Another day I had my timings all worked out to go meet a friend, but found that as I went to scoop Lexi out of her swing that she had soaked herself through with vomit. It took fifteen minutes to clean her up, resulting in me being fifteen minutes late.

I am gradually learning to build in buffer time for everything now, from writing this book to getting out of the house to have coffee with a friend. Just as, pre-baby, I would allow fudge factor between meetings or to make a flight, I'm mentally readjusting all my timings to allow for child-related delays. When I manage to do this successfully and a delay hits, I'm not stressing about running late. And when no delay eventuates, I'm early for the appointment.

A recent HuffPost article aimed to help readers build more buffer time into their days. One of the easiest ways to do this, it said, was to allow extra travel time to and from appointments, and to schedule fewer tasks per day.

Children by their very nature are quintessential curve balls – and curve balls are the ultimate wet blanket on any attempts to be organised. The objective is to build some infrastructure around those curve balls, so that when they do what they do, the impact is as limited as possible.

The GRO list

1. Make a list of everyone who is part of your family life support team and identify what each of them contributes to help you do what you do.

2. Make a list of all the responsibilities you currently manage for the family, and try to spot which ones you could outsource using the Time Task Audit worksheet.

3. Choose one system – no matter how small – that's in operation right now for your family, and consider the impact of not having that system. How does it help your family?

4. Identify three 'stones in your shoe' when it comes to family life, and brainstorm what system could be put in place to remedy them.

5. Write down what morning and evening routines look like right now for your family. Ask yourself if there are ways you could improve on them.

6. Put in place a communication structure with your support team if you haven't got one already.

7. Think about a situation where your children created a curve ball. What fudge factor could you have built in to prevent that happening again?

CHAPTER 14

The endstate

We have spent quite a bit of time together, you and I, discussing various tactics we can employ to get back in the driving seat of our lives by becoming remarkably organised.

We have covered decluttering, standards, routines, planning our weeks, managing our days, conquering distractions, outsourcing, overcoming procrastination and making it work with little people. We've covered a lot of ground together!

Having been on this journey so far, it's timely to check in with what the outcome of being remarkably organised is – how does it serve us, ultimately, when we pull this off successfully?

Way back in the introductory chapter, as we started this journey together, we spoke about the concept of intent, and how it has three distinct elements: purpose, method and endstate.

I asked you to identify what your *purpose* was for picking up this book – you alone will know that.

I've provided you with a *method* via the various concepts and ideas we have walked through together in these chapters.

At the outset, I also asked you to articulate what the *endstate* would be for you personally, having successfully implemented the method in your life. Take a moment now to check in with that endstate as a reminder to you on where you want to be, and also as extra motivation as you begin to embed these structures into your life.

There are four broader wins that I see as part of the endstate of having our shit together on the organisational front.

1. We're in flow

Being in a state of flow is one of the best feelings *ever*. We have the time and headspace to concentrate on the task at hand. Distractions are non-existent, and even if they're there, they seem to bounce off the forcefield of our focus. The work feels almost effortless. We lose track of time. We forget to eat or go to the bathroom.

For me, being in this state is blissful. I know with every fibre of my being that what I'm doing is valuable work, and I feel grateful to be able to focus on it so fully. I'm in this state while writing this chapter right now.

Writing these words is my second MIT for the day – the first was mapping out the chapter in advance. Even though my to-do list for today is pretty hefty, I've got enough time allocated in my time plan (including baby buffer time!) to tick off everything on my list.

I know that writing this chapter is getting me closer to my goals, as having a second book published is one of my objectives for the year. Therefore I'm in a state of enjoyment rather than pleasure, as author of *Flow*, Mihaly Csikszentmihalyi, would say.

Being in flow isn't relegated to writing or other creative pursuits. I can get in flow while cooking a meal, going for a walk or having a strategy session with the team. It's a sense of being fully present in what I'm doing, and knowing that what I'm doing is productive.

Being able to achieve a state of flow is, for me, one of the greatest benefits that comes from being organised. It's the dual win of knowing that what I'm doing is worthwhile while also knowing that the time has been managed so that I focus fully on it.

Having that opportunity for full focus is what being remarkably organised is all about for me – it's the carrot at the end of all the planning, list writing and tiny habits performed daily.

2. We can actually have 'off' time

Being organised should not involve us feeling we should be doing something constantly. In fact, it's the very opposite!

When we're organised, we have a clear visual of what we want to do, and we have sufficient time and energy to complete our tasks in the time we allocate to them. The net result of this is that when we have time to relax, we can actually *relax*.

When we're *not* organised, we feel behind the eight ball and like we're in a constant state of catch-up. We never seem to get the chance to chill out, as there's always something that needs to be done – and usually it's urgent as we should have done it a week earlier.

We might procrastinate about a task, which means that even when we're meant to be having fun, we feel guilty because we should be working on that task. I don't know about you, but that 'I should be working on X' feeling is an absolute buzz killer!

The feeling of really having earned the right to check into Rancho Relaxo, because we're making serious headway on our plan for the week, is the absolute best, and having that feeling regularly is a major part of my personal target endstate.

> Having downtime is also key to ensuring our ability to stay organised long-term.

I do not believe that going full tilt for weeks on end is sustainable, and it's also not when we do our best work. It's essential that we rest and reset by building relaxation into our weekly plans.

Dale Carnegie told a story of a pair of men who were out chopping wood. One man worked hard all day and took no breaks except to stop briefly for lunch. The other man took several breaks during the day and had a short nap at lunch time.

At the end of the day, the man who had taken no breaks was quite disturbed to see that his companion had cut more wood than he had. He said, 'I don't understand. Every time I looked around, you were sitting down, yet you cut more wood than I did.' His companion asked, 'Did you also notice that while I was sitting down, I was sharpening my axe?'

The analogy of 'sharpening our axe' is, of course, relevant to planning. However, it also speaks to the importance of adequate rest.

When I'm doing something relaxing like a yoga class or a big Sunday cook-up, my brain is processing all the information it took in during the week when I was engaged in business strategy, writing or other tasks. Giving it the chance to rest means that it will fire up easily when I next need to work on a big task, and I'll feel more refreshed and energised as well.

Just this morning, I decided to go for a walk rather than starting on this chapter first thing. There was torrential rain all day yesterday, and I was craving sunshine, fresh air and movement. While it seemed counter-intuitive to not get stuck into writing straight away, the walk was of great benefit as I felt reset and my writing flowed easily as a result.

3. We work towards self-mastery

Self-mastery is probably the most valuable thing we can focus on to get closer to the life of our dreams. When we move from being at the mercy of external forces (people, events, circumstances) and instead concentrate on mastering ourselves, getting what we want out of life is inevitable. It's the process of moving from being reactive to proactive that Steven Covey talks about in *The Seven Habits of Highly Effective People*.

Successfully executing our own personal recipe for feeling organised is in itself an achievement. In order to do this well, we need to develop and continuously engage several aspects of self-mastery, including willpower, discipline, focus and commitment.

I'm sure I'm not alone in feeling extremely accomplished when I have a clear plan set for the week, when I discipline myself to stay on track with my MITs or when I successfully ingrain a new habit into my routine.

> Relatively small triumphs positively reinforce our own self-belief, and set us up for bigger successes in our lives.

In particular, the willpower we develop in doing so serves us on many levels. As Kelly McGonigal writes in *The Willpower Instinct*: 'Just as it's possible to train your arm muscle through weight lifting, it's possible to train your willpower muscle with willpower challenges. By performing small but regular willpower challenges you can gradually improve your self control.'

> Once you become the master of yourself, the world doesn't stand a chance!

4. We're happier

This is the endstate that all of us seek, I'm sure. If my life is in order, I feel happier. It's that simple.

When I attended an event with Tony Robbins a few years ago, he said that 'Happiness equals progress.'

Could it really be that simple?

I think it can.

I am at my happiest when I feel like I'm making progress. This is certainly true in a business sense – when we win a new client, when a new strategy is taking shape, when the team feels like it's really pulling together.

However, it also holds true for other areas of my life. I feel

I'm making progress when my muscles are more defined after regular yoga practice, when I have a really good chat with a friend and I feel our friendship is developing, when Wade and I have a great day out together and collect another memory for our relationship.

Now, watching Lexi develop each day is a huge source of happiness. By bearing witness to her progress, it makes all of us around her happy as well.

> The very nature of being organised is that our lives are focused on progress – which can't *help but* make us happier!

My closing words to you

This is the time in the book where I leave you with some upbeat, motivating words to send you on your way into organisational bliss.

I'm not sure how motivating I plan on being, as what I'd rather do is reassure you at this point. There are some things I'd like you to be cognisant of as you work through each chapter and bring the concepts to life.

Do what works for you

Rather than seeing this book as a must-eat-everything degustation, see it as a tasting platter from which you can choose which dishes are most appealing to you personally. What is heaven to you might be hell to another, so give something a red hot go – and if it doesn't work for you, no problem! Just find something that works for you. The most important thing is that you *stick* with what works for you.

Remember it's a constantly evolving beast

If I wrote another version of this book next year, the ideas I would suggest might be quite different. That's not to say the essential principles would change – I don't think they would; however, the tools I engage at any one time are right for where my life is at that point. Don't be surprised if something that works a treat for you right now doesn't have the same impact in a few months' time.

As our lives progress, we'll need to tweak the organisational infrastructure we employ to help us operate at our highest potential. The trick is to ebb and flow with where your life is at, and be flexible in your approach to it.

Layer, layer, layer

It's likely that you're sick of hearing me say this, but I really can't overestimate the importance of taking a slow and steady approach to building more organisation into your life. Taking small consistent steps every day is undoubtedly of more value than big occasional leaps. You are significantly more likely to stay the course by building small, repetitive actions into each day than by undertaking a big-ass effort a couple of times a week.

Treat yourself

Self-incentivising has been a common thread on our journey together so far. This is for one very simple reason: it works. In time, you'll reap the 'deeper' rewards of investing in becoming remarkably organised – you'll be achieving more of your goals in less time, and you'll have a deep-seated sense of accomplishment.

Compare this journey you're on to a similar journey to get fit.

In the early days, you're ticking off the gym sessions and early morning starts with little to show for them. A couple of weeks in, you start to notice some subtle changes. A month in and you can see the evidence of your training in your muscle definition, and you may have lost a little weight. At that point, you can tangibly see – and feel – the pay-off for all your hard work and the need for mini-rewards has probably dwindled.

Self-incentivising with little treats as you get your organisational mission underway will help you stay on track, as well as help you to embed new habits gradually. The feeling of profound accomplishment will come as you get into the driving seat of your life, but in the meantime perks like chocolate, walks, wine and Netflix will keep you going.

Remember that no one is perfect

Including me – I regularly slip up with how I organise my life. I have days when I don't tick one thing off my to-do list, go a week without practising my morning routine and find myself doing low-value tasks that are most certainly not what I should be focusing my time on.

Author Sarah Wilson advises those who slip up on her 'I Quit Sugar' program to eat a pork chop. One reason is that the fat and protein in the pork helps to stabilise blood sugar. However, another – and greater – reason is that it gives the person a proactive course of action to deal with the inevitable slip-up.

The beauty of this solution is that rather than being in a disempowered state berating themselves for eating sugar (and probably eating even more sugar to make themselves feel better), the person switches into an empowered state by completing a specific action – eating the pork chop.

When you experience an organisational slip-up, don't use it as an opportunity to beat yourself up. Instead, focus your energy on doing one of these things:

1. Do a ten-minute tidy-up of a room in your house or your workspace.
2. Write your to-do list for tomorrow.
3. Go for a ten-minute walk around the block with the express intention of hitting your brain's 'reset' button.
4. Read ten pages of a book.
5. Read the most relevant troubleshooting topic from the next part of this book.

Buddy up

It can be extraordinarily helpful to have someone come along on this journey with you. This might be your partner, a friend, a sibling or a work colleague. Having someone alongside you will help you stay accountable and will make the whole experience more fun. It's also nice to have someone who is in the trenches with you and therefore knows first hand how much work has gone into something – those high fives are a lot more valuable, I've found!

See if there's someone in your life who is also keen to get more shape into their life. Pass this book on to them and have regular check-ins on how you're tracking with everything from your one-day declutters to chalking up wins on your to-do lists.

If you'd like to connect with other readers of this book, join us on Facebook in our 'Get Remarkably Organised' group.

Share your wins with me

I adore hearing how people are implementing my tips and tricks into their lives! Please do drop me a line to share how you're doing, and ask me any questions that might come up for you.

lorrainemurphy.com.au
⃝ @lorraineremarks
🅕 /lorraineremarks

TROUBLESHOOTING

Introduction

Welcome to Part Two of the book!

If you're here, you probably fall into one of three camps:

1. You've picked this book up and flicked straight to the fix-my-problem-lady section.
2. You've smashed the 'theory' and associated exercises, and are keen to pick up any other little gems coming your way.
3. You read the book a while ago, and are back now with a specific problem.

The challenges I'm addressing are based on the biggest ones I've faced in getting and keeping my life in order, observing challenges faced by my team and mentees, asking those around me, and seeking input via social media. Whichever camp you're in, or whatever challenge you're facing, my wish is that this section will help you.

When approaching these challenges, I'm putting my 'mentor' hat on. I'm imagining you as one of my mentees – and considering what simple, speedy steps I would suggest to them to get out of the funk they are in. I can imagine that you don't want a whole lot of background info right now – you want to get on with fixing the problem you're dealing with (or maybe not dealing with!) right now.

As a result, this troubleshooting section is very action orientated. I'm giving you a simple menu of ways in which you could tackle the issues you're having, based on my own experience of them and seeing how others have overcome them before.

Right, let's get started.

1. I'm just too fucking busy

Change your language

When we're busy, we often tell ourselves how crazy-busy we are – 'Wow, today's a busy day' or 'Holy crap I'm busy'. Then we tell *other* people how busy we are.

> Them: 'How are you?'
> Us: 'Oh you know, SO BUSY!'

An alien landing on Planet Earth could be excused for thinking that 'busy' is some kind of sickness from which these earthlings seem to suffer. We live in a culture where the busier we are, the more important we are.

It's absolute bollocks.

Observe how much the word 'busy' is creeping into not only your self-talk but also your conversations with others. My friend Melissa Ambrosini weaned herself off the word 'busy' a few years ago, and replaced it with the word 'full'.

'Full' is a much more positive word, and if you believe in vibrations like I do, it's vibrating at a much higher frequency than 'busy'. When I replace describing my day as 'busy' with 'full', it makes me feel very different.

The word 'full' suggests abundance, like our cup runneth over with so much good stuff. Having a 'full' schedule also gives us more control over it. 'Busy' feels external to us, like we have no say in how busy we get. 'Full' gives us more control. After all, if a cup is too full we simply tip a little liquid out!

Start by changing your language. You are no longer too busy; your schedule is full.

And full we can do something about.

Analyse how you spent your time in the last fourteen days

Quite often, I've found that doing some cold analysis of where I'm spending my time will throw up some pretty confronting insights on why I'm not feeling like I'm getting ahead.

Wade and I decided to go back to the start of *Game of Thrones* when Lexi arrived, and so far I've banked sixty hours of watching it in the last two months. This is fine; however, when I wonder why my evenings don't feel as productive, I've got a pretty solid reason right there!

You can do this analysis retrospectively by using your diary and guesstimating some approximate timings, or there are a number of tools that you can use to track your timing on an ongoing basis, including Toggl, RescueTime and Timr.

Identify what time is time well spent

I think we'd all agree that Sir Richard Branson is a pretty important person – yet when I spent time with him, I was struck by how present he was in what he was doing. He never once talked about how busy he was, how long his to-do list was, or how much work must have been banking up while he took the time to be with our group on Necker Island.

I've noticed this common trait among truly successful people – they're not busy, they're spending time doing the things that they should be doing to continue being successful.

If you feel like you've got too many commitments and are not moving closer to your goals, then you need to have a good look at what is taking up all your time – and decide whether that's helping you or not.

Look at where you spent your time in the last fortnight, and ask yourself honestly if you would be closer to achieving your goals and being happier if you spent the next fifty-two weeks like the last fourteen days.

Remember that progress equals happiness – and if your current schedule isn't enabling you to progress, then you need to address that now. Not tomorrow, now!

Subtract some commitments

I often think that someone's ability to gracefully extricate themselves from commitments – and politely decline them in the first place – is a hallmark of someone who is really going places. It sends a clear signal to me that this person values their own time, and as a result I value their time more.

I've had some amazing people say no to me – and they do it so elegantly that I hardly even notice that they've refused me!

> Be one of those people who are selective about what they take on. Your success depends on it.

Make a list of the commitments you have tended to over the last fourteen days and rank them in order of importance. Have a very careful think about whether those commitments that are ranking lowest are worthy of your time now, and in the future.

No matter how untenable, daunting or downright scary it might be to withdraw from an existing commitment, go there in your mind's eye and feel how much time and energy subtracting it might free up for you.

As author and entrepreneur Zoe Foster-Blake said, 'I love saying no to things, as it means I'm saying yes to myself.'

Prevent this feeling in future

When saying yes to commitments going forward, consider your Future Self before you say yes.

I've been guilty of booking a holiday and assuming that Future Lorraine will have oodles of disposable income by then to live it up. I'm equally guilty of saying yes to an interstate speaking gig in six months' time, again assuming that Future Lorraine will have three days of free time just begging to be filled. The speaking gig rolls around and – *quelle surprise!* – Future Lorraine has just as full a schedule (if not more full) than Past Lorraine.

Take a good old spoonful of Reality before admitting new commitments into your diary to prevent overwhelming your Future Self.

2. I'm utterly overwhelmed

Get some sleep

I know this sounds ridiculously counter-intuitive right now; however, as we've already covered earlier in this book, being very tired is not too dissimilar to being very drunk. I know from hard-won personal experience that there is a direct correlation between how tired I am and how overwhelmed I am.

> Everything – and I mean everything – feels harder when we're missing out on sleep.

Commit to getting an early night tonight, cancel some plans for tomorrow night so you can rest, or go crazy and have a twenty-minute power nap right now. The optimal time for a rebooting nap is twenty minutes – which I promise will be time well spent if you wake up feeling a little more rested and less overwhelmed.

Write a list

It may be the longest mofo list you've ever seen, but write it anyway. Having 'stuff we need to do' rattling around in our brains is exhausting, and feeds the Overwhelm Monster.

These things can be big (update our résumé, paint the living room) or small (book a table for dinner, cancel health insurance). The problem arises when we don't capture them somewhere, so even a little two-minute job like making a restaurant reservation feels like an epic task once it has boomeranged back into our minds for the tenth time that week.

Write.

It.

Down.

All.

Of.

It.

When I sense I'm in overwhelm territory, I generally freak out for a few days. You know, just being overwhelmed. When the pain gets too much, I finally dig deep and write a list.

This involves taking a page in my notebook and writing headings down for each area of my life. The headings normally read like this:

- The Remarkables Group
- Remarkability (my speaking, mentoring and writing)
- house
- finance
- health
- admin
- travel.

Then under each heading I write a list of the things I need to do within that area. It's essentially vomiting all the swirly thoughts in my head onto a structured page.

Once all the to-dos are on there, I am immediately calmer. I've probably done this process twenty times over the last few years, and never once has the list felt more difficult than my mind and its swirly thoughts would have had me believe. Getting everything down on paper is the first step towards me getting back in control of where I'm at in that moment.

Once the list is done, I go through each item one by one and see whether it's something I can delegate or else outsource (i.e. pay for it to go away). Then for everything remaining, I write a day next to it when I'll complete that task.

Lastly, I will do *at least one action* on that list before I get up from my desk. It might be sending an email to someone on my team asking them to look after something, setting up a meeting to get a big project moving, making the thirty-second phone call to book a hair appointment, or cancelling my plans for the following evening so I have time to catch my breath. This makes me feel that I'm already winning, and some equilibrium returns.

Tidy somewhere

I know it sounds rather counter-intuitive to spend ten minutes tidying up when your to-do list is already overflowing. Bear with me!

By physically organising an area – no matter how small that area is – we reclaim a sense of control over our surroundings, and in doing so, our mental state. A second advantage to doing this is the 'white space' it creates. Sorting through tangible items helps us to sort through our thoughts as well; it essentially gives us a breather from being overwhelmed that still feels like it's constructive. Let's call it therapeutic tidying!

I find tidying up our daughter's clothes to be very calming. I have no idea why, but if I'm feeling upset or overwhelmed, ten minutes of sorting through and folding tiny clothes is extraordinarily effective at helping me reach a more balanced equilibrium.

Have a blitz

When the house was starting to tip into chaos when we were kids, my mum would commit to a 'blitz on the house'. This involved my parents, my sister and me each having a list of tasks that needed to get done in the next few hours – for example, my tasks might be vacuuming the house and putting away laundry. After about three hours of full-on action, the house was back in order and we all had a terrific sense of accomplishment.

I love the idea of having a set amount of time for massive action – a big burst of productivity that you know you'll have a sense of accomplishment at the end of. This is precisely why the Marie Kondo style of decluttering works so well.

Sometimes one or two items on our to-do list can eclipse all the other things, and they become chronic blocks to us getting to all the other stuff we need to do – not to mention inducing adrenalin-fuelled panics in the middle of the night.

If there is one big item on your list that is especially sending you into overwhelmed mode, commit to spending a morning/afternoon/evening on it to get it moving. It always amazes me how much I can achieve on a chunky task when I give myself a couple of hours to get some momentum on it.

It's getting that snowball made and starting it rolling down the hill. Once it's rolling, you'll have a tailwind behind you that will make completing the task a hell of a lot easier.

Get some help

I have become a lot better at recognising the signs that I'm starting to sink rather than swim since my brush with burn-out eighteen months after I started the business (you can read all about Black November in my first book).

One of the first things I do now when I feel I'm slipping under is to draft in some help. This might be having a big brain dump of how I'm feeling with Wade, or booking in a top-up session with my kinesiologist/ energy healer Jacqui. For you, it might be a few glasses of cab sauv with a friend who's an awesome listener, a session with a mentor or a preventative chat with a therapist – whatever works for you.

Having a healthy way (isn't red wine good for your heart?!) to release the build-up of tension when we're overwhelmed is essential in getting us back on an even keel quickly, acting like a release valve on a pressure cooker. So book something in now that will help you recalibrate – both mentally and emotionally.

3. I can't stop procrastinating

Read Chapter 12. I wrote it just for you.

4. I'm not inspired/excited by what I'm doing

This is a very real problem for many of us; I've been there myself quite a few times. And it sucks.

Getting up day after day and not looking forward to what's ahead of us is absolutely soul-destroying. It kills our motivation, leaves us feeling all over the place and leads us to be precisely the opposite of remarkably organised.

We seek out pleasurable activities (shopping, eating, partying) to distract ourselves from what's going on, and enjoyable activities (i.e. ones that get us closer to our goals) are a rarity or non-existent.

This is not the book to tackle this particular problem in detail – there are many, many books written by people far smarter and more worldly-wise than me on that topic; however, here are a few steps I've personally taken to get myself out of an uninspired rut.

Get real with yourself

Every single morning, Steve Jobs would ask himself: 'If today were my last day, would I want to do what I'm about to do today?' If the answer was 'no' too many mornings in a row, then he would make some changes.

If you're not inspired by the life you're living, it's time to ask yourself some serious questions. And time to answer them honestly.

Listen to your heart. Or your gut.

Both these organs have served me very well in the past. Just last year I made a radical decision to completely pivot the model of The Remarkables Group.

I had known that the model we were offering was not the best solution to brands for months; however, I was too afraid to acknowledge that – even to myself. On some level (gut, heart), I knew there was a major change I needed to make, but to be very honest with you, I was shit scared.

Changing the model made no sense on a financial level (representing influencers had brought in $2 million in the previous financial year) or a strategic level (we already had a perfectly viable model). However, my heart knew that I wasn't happy, and my gut told me that we could make a real go of a new model.

So I did it. I decided to resign all the talent we represented and instead focus on providing unbiased strategic advice to brands.

It was the best thing I could have done for the business. And you know what? I'm so much happier and cannot wait to get stuck in every day.

Commit to doing one thing

Identify one thing that would improve your situation, and commit to doing one thing that will inch you closer to where you want to be. It might be updating your résumé so you can apply for a new job, finally calling time on a flailing relationship or finding a web designer to create a website for the new venture you've been wanting to start.

Making that commitment to action will direct your energy in a constructive direction and completing just one task will gain you some momentum as you get started (remember the snowball).

5. All my little tasks are getting in the way of the important stuff

Prioritise

Setting your priorities in line with the importance of the tasks at hand is crucial in helping you to get started on those bigger or scarier tasks.

Those tasks will generally be the ones that are going to get you closer to the life you want to be living.

The number-one suggestion I have for you to get more out of your days is to do the big/scary/important stuff FIRST. That stuff will get you closer to where you want to be in your life, and that's why it's often harder to start with getting those tasks done. As Steven Pressfield said, we resist getting started on a task more as the difficulty or importance of that task increases.

Write that important task as the first MIT (Most Important Task) on your to-do list, and employ every ounce of self-discipline you have to sit down and get that done first tomorrow morning. Ensure that you have the time to make some solid inroads on it, block out all distractions (Chapter 10 will help you with that) and GET IT DONE. This does get easier over time as our brains flex their willpower muscle.

Write a list

Sometimes it can feel like we have a lot more little tasks when they're being given free rein to float around our brains. Getting them all down on paper puts them in clear focus, and we can start to deal with them properly.

Write down all those finicky little tasks you have floating around – yep, every single one of them!

Next, rank them in order of importance, on a scale of 1 to 10. Is filing your tax return a 5 or a 9? Is returning a friend's tennis racket a 1 or a 7? You will know yourself the importance and urgency that each task has.

Then circle the tasks that are *really* time critical – the ones that, if you don't do them, you'll be sailing your way up shit creek. These are the tasks that you need to prioritise.

Make 'small task time' an MIT

When I realise that important and urgent little tasks are building up like this, I'll schedule some time to work through them as an MIT. This will generally involve grouping a bunch of them together and allowing an hour to rattle through as many of them as I can. Ticking off a few in one session gives me a good sense of achievement, and I don't feel I'm 'wasting' an MIT by devoting it to small tasks.

6. I'm spending all my time in meetings and have no time to get work done

Realise that you ARE still working

For many of us, being out with our 'publics' is the most valuable work we can be doing. We often fall into the trap of thinking that because we're not sitting at our desks frantically tapping away like caffeinated monkeys, we're not working. I know that, personally, the hours I spend in meetings with my clients, team and advisers represent the best use of my time.

So, first off, remember that you are working when you're pressing the flesh in whatever role it is you do.

Offload unnecessary meetings

The problem arises when we're sitting in meetings that we *know to our core* are not productive or useful. I abhor this feeling, when I am terrifyingly aware that my time is being wasted – not to mention the time of everyone sitting there in the meeting with me.

You will have varying levels of control over the number of meetings at which you need to be present – this will be dictated by your customers and managers. I know I am fortunate that, as a business owner, I have more say than some people in what meetings I choose to allow into my diary.

Review your diary over the last fortnight and identify which meetings were genuinely not productive, and were abetting rather than aiding your ability to get shit done. Write each meeting along the left-hand side of a page.

Next, ask yourself why that meeting was a waste of time. For example:

- Was it because there was no clear agenda?
- Was it because the discussion was not relevant to your role?
- Was it because the person with whom you were meeting wasn't a decision-maker?
- Was it because it was a recurring meeting, and everyone had kind of forgotten why it had been held in the first place?
- Was the meeting being run unproductively – for example, were participants giving long-winded updates that frequently go off on tangents?
- Was it because you got a meeting invite, and once you got there you had no fucking idea why the invitee thought you'd need to be there?

Identifying exactly why you feel your meetings are time-wasting is the first step to dealing with them.

Next to each meeting that you've listed on your page, create a second column and write the reason why you think it was a waste of time.

Now we need to decide what you can do about it. As I said, your scope may be limited here – if, for example, you work with a major global corporate or you're currently sitting on one of the lower rungs of the seniority ladder. Even if that is the case, you can have influence over your own personal sphere of behaviour.

If you find you're attending meetings you're genuinely not required for, can you politely extricate yourself from them?

If a particular meeting is going on and on and ON, can you gently steer the conversation back to the agenda, or be mindful of keeping your own updates succinct in the hope that others will follow your lead?

Work through the items on your list one by one and write down an action you could take for that particular meeting – remembering that small steps lead to big steps.

Book out no-meeting time

This trick is essential for anyone working for a corporate, where it can sometimes feel that people have meetings about having meetings! You may find that you've been saving Thursday morning to actually get some work done, and all of a sudden on Wednesday afternoon three meetings get dropped into your already-heaving schedule.

As part of your weekly planning session, book in blocks of time where you know you'll be able to get your head down and bang out some tasks. It's up to you how creative you want to get with labelling this time if colleagues also have access to your calendar!

Compartmentalise meetings

I am a stickler for not doing meetings at all on a Monday, and only having internal meetings on a Friday. In fact, I can't imagine having my week any other way after running it like this for about three years now.

We talked in Chapter 8 about being on a Maker's schedule versus a Manager's schedule. Mondays and Fridays are my days to 'make', and Tuesday to Thursday I pack in as many (useful) meetings as I can.

I used to make the mistake of thinking I had to have all of my time available for meetings – especially when the business was in its younger days. I thought that when someone suggested a meeting time that it would be rude not to say yes immediately.

I have become adept at sending a polite response, saying 'I can't do Monday, how about Tuesday?'. I don't need to explain that I don't have any other meetings on Monday, all the other person needs to know is that I can't meet that day.

Use a Maker vs Manager lens on your week and run a few experiments to see how it works for you.

Allow for meeting action time

I shared in Chapter 8 how I have begun allowing buffer time after certain meetings to tick off the actions arising in that meeting quickly – for example, my monthly finance meeting with our financial controller.

If there are meetings that you know will result in you having a series of tasks to complete, try allowing 30–60 minutes immediately after them to get those tasks done. It's immeasurably easier to tackle them when everything is still fresh in our minds and we've got momentum from just stepping out of the meeting.

It crushes my motivation when I have 'finance meeting actions' sitting on my to-do list for a week. I can hardly remember what we spoke about four days earlier, and the resistance steadily builds day after day until those actions become something about which I procrastinate. In total contrast, when I smash them immediately after the meeting, I'm on fire!

7. I'm constantly distracted

That is your own fault. I told you I'd be speaking to you like I do to my mentees! (#toughlove)

When we go down a path of blaming other people/emails/kids for distracting us, we are in a disempowered state.

When we get a grip on the situation and realise that it starts, begins and ends with us being empowered to do something about it, *then* we can resolve the problem.

Your time is your own, and no one else's. Therefore, it's up to you to cherish, use and fiercely protect that time.

Turn to Chapter 10, where I go into the topic of distraction in detail and give you plenty of ideas on how you can manage it.

8. I started so well, now I've fallen off the wagon

It's okay

Please don't beat yourself up. It's a pointless waste of energy.

Remember that even the very best/smartest/coolest people in the universe get off track sometimes, and what matters is that you're trying.

Please also remember that 'failure' is just feedback. We just need to tweak things a little to get you firing on all organisational cylinders again.

Get back in touch with your why

Discussing our 'why' has become so very *de rigeur* in recent times – thanks to the awesome genius that is Simon Sinek.

At the start of this book, I asked you, my remarkable reader, to articulate clearly what your purpose was for picking up this book and getting started on your journey to getting remarkably organised.

Consider what that purpose is again – why do you want to get your life more in order? How will you feel once you're back in the driving seat? What benefits will you see from being more organised? How will the lives of those around you be positively impacted?

Remembering *why* we want to do something is the first step to getting back on the wagon and keeping up all our great work.

What went wrong?

Something triggered you to fall off the wagon. Maybe you went away for the weekend and didn't get a chance to do your weekly planning session. Or work got totally crazy and your to-do list approach got forgotten in the manic rush to keep up with the demands coming your way. Or your child was sick and, rather than doing Miracle Mornings, you instead found yourself doing Survival Mornings.

Figure out what it was that went wrong and resulted in you falling off the organisational wagon. Now identify one thing you could do to prevent that happening again.

It may be that you're attempting to take on too much too quickly. In that case, strip a couple of things out, master the basics, then layer them back in again.

Reward yourself for what you are doing well

I'm pretty sure that there are some things you are doing super-well, so make sure you're rewarding yourself for those things.

Rewards are key to helping us positively reinforce new behaviours with ourselves – after all, if a puppy gets a harsh word, even when they're doing good things, do you think they'll keep up that behaviour? Of course not!

'Puppy train' yourself with small treats that help you to stay the course and don't fall into the trap of holding off rewarding yourself until the very end of a big task. Getting more organised is a constantly evolving process – a process we never 'finish'.

Get an accountability buddy

It may be of great benefit to you to buddy up with someone else who can help you stay accountable. There are tonnes of studies showing how people maintained a regular exercise habit because they had a friend doing it with them. Avoiding letting our friend down is a seriously good motivator to help us get out of bed on a cold winter morning for that run!

The person doesn't even need to have the same goal as you for this to be effective. I remember reading an interview with a writer who was procrastinating about starting his book. He emailed a former boss of his to tell him that he had to have the book written by a certain date, and if he hadn't written it by then he instructed the ex-boss to call him and bawl him out. Knowing that he had a) put the goal out there and b) that someone he looked up to was going to be disappointed if he didn't do it meant he met his self-imposed deadline.

Find someone who will talk straight to you and tell them what you're aiming to do, then ask them to check in daily or weekly with you to make sure that you're on track. If they want to join you on your goals, even better.

Another way you could get some accountability going would be to join a group – in fact, I have started a 'Get Remarkably Organised' group on Facebook for that exact purpose. Sharing your weekly goals – even with people you have never met – will give you added glue to keep you on your path.

9. I'm drowning in admin

Oh gawd, I hear you on this one! As I shared earlier in the book, admin – especially personal admin – makes me itchy.

Dealing with phone accounts, insurance claims, postage, banking and all manner of admin drives me insane. First, it's not getting me closer to my goals and therefore feels like a gigantic waste of time. Second, some of it simply can't be delegated as it's my name on the various accounts. Third, I have no option but to do it. Otherwise I'll find myself in all manner of unpleasant situations (namely late fees, lost money, legal bills).

This shit never goes away – so I've learned a few coping strategies to help me deal with it.

Make a list

Ah, our friend the list saves the day again!

Making a list of all the admin I need to deal with immediately lets me set some parameters on it. So I brain dump all the crappy admin tasks I need to do in a mofo boring list in my notebook.

I don't bother going through this particular list asking which is going to get me closer to my goals because – let's face it – none of it is. *sad face*

Instead I number them in order of urgency. The pet insurance claim could probably wait a bit, but updating my gym account with my new credit card details probably can't wait, as my membership has already bounced once.

Once there's a list in order of priority, we can start tackling it.

Admin Power Hour

I don't know about you, but if I have an entire day of dealing with admin shit, I a) will be as miserable AF, and b) I probably won't do it. In fact, I'll probably do everything else *but* the admin.

Allocating one hour purely to dealing with this list is a manageable way to approach it. It gives us enough time to (hopefully) tick two or three items off, but it's not so long that we start to lose our minds.

It's pretty simple. We commit to dealing with our admin list for the next sixty minutes and start with the most urgent task first. When the hour is up, we cross off the things we have managed to do, and when our next Admin Power Hour rolls around, we pick up where we left off.

Automate what you can

Where possible, find ways to automate your admin so that you can save your Future Self the headache of dealing with it.

One of my mentees, Emily Harper, had a monthly task of paying all the bills for her business. The bills would come in paper form to her salon, she would file them together and once a month she would go into the salon with the sole purpose of checking through them, logging into her online banking and paying each bill. This task would take roughly three hours to do each month and – as you can imagine – she didn't exactly love doing it.

One day she decided that there must be an easier way to do it. She set herself a task of automating as much of it as she could. She worked through each of her regular bills and set up online accounts for as many of them as possible. She then filled out the authorisation for direct debits for them. And lastly, she set recurring reminders in her diary for the dates the bills were due to hit, so she could make sure there was enough funds in the account to cover them before the amount was debited.

With 90 per cent of her payments now running automatically, she had rid herself of a chunky (and highly boring) task each month.

Look at the admin burden you're currently shouldering and see how you could cut it down using some smart automation. You might be surprised at how much you can get rid of!

10. My email inbox is driving me insane

Employ the use of 'found time'

One of my friends, Toby Dewar, has a senior role at a major bank and three children. He spends most of his days in meetings and when he's home, he wants to be present with his kids.

He uses his train commute to and from the office to deal with his inbox – meaning he can attend his meetings during the day knowing that his messages have been dealt with, and be present with his family in the evenings and at weekends.

This kind of time is what I call 'found time'. It's time that would otherwise be 'lost time'; however, by engaging instead in productive tasks, we find multiple pockets of minutes every day that would otherwise be lost.

Look at your average day and spot opportunities for 'found time'. It might be the ten minutes you spend waiting for the kids at school pick-up, the five minutes queuing for service at the post office or even the three minutes while you're waiting for your next appointment.

Setting a goal of clearing X number of emails in that time means that gradually throughout the day, you can clear your inbox using time that would otherwise be lost to you.

Consider deleting the lot of them

I set an email auto-responder on the day I stepped back from the business to go on maternity leave, stating that I was currently in Baby Land and giving a couple of different contacts who people could reach while I was there.

I was probably in my inbox daily with the exception of the week immediately after Lexi arrived, and responded to the urgent emails when

I was. I wasn't as fastidious as I normally would be in deleting emails, so when it came time – just last week – to switch off my out-of-office, I had built up 300 emails in my inbox.

It was an option to go through each of them and find the ones I still needed to respond to; however, that would take at least half a day to do and that time simply wasn't available to me. I knew that anyone who had emailed would have received the auto-response, and if their request was urgent that they would email me again. So I hit the 'select all' box and deleted the lot of them.

I started the day with a clean slate and banished any guilt for not responding to every email.

When you finally get back to your desk after a holiday, the ultimate kicker back into reality is a bursting inbox. Ditto for returning from a few days of conference or training – you're rearing to get started on a new plan or action list, but instead you're faced with a mountain of emails. You spend your first day back responding to them, and by the end of the day your morning sparkiness has dissipated into the ether.

There is a growing trend for people to expressly tell others that if they're sending an email in a certain period, it will be deleted.

Wade heard a story recently of someone who was going away for a few weeks and set their out-of-office with the subject line 'Your email has been deleted'. The body of the auto-responder went on to explain that due to the high volume of emails the person received, the emails they received while they were away would automatically be deleted. If the query was still relevant after the date when the person returned, they were asked to resend the email then.

Incredibly, only 20 per cent of people re-sent their email – meaning that this clever person essentially cut out the need to deal with 80 per cent of the inbox they could have had. Amazing!

Schedule email management time

Email management is one of those strange tasks that needs to be done every day, but is so invisible that it never makes it onto our to-do lists as a task in its own right. As a result, we might spend two hours responding to emails but it doesn't feel like productive time as we can't tick anything off our list after that sizeable amount of time.

I find it much more satisfying to identify emails for what they are – another task – and, as such, include them as a to-do list item when I'm writing my list for the day. This means I can more accurately manage my time for the day, and I get the satisfaction of crossing the task off my list. It also means that there are some parameters around my email management, and I don't feel I need to be doing that task constantly throughout the day.

Employ a one-touch system

I talked about this system in detail in *Remarkability*. It essentially involves touching our emails just once.

We might normally open an email, read it and then decide to deal with it later. This means that we are essentially double-handling that email, which means increased workload physically (having to deal with it) but also mentally (having to think about dealing with it a second time).

What is infinitely more effective is disciplining ourselves to touch emails just once. There will be four actions we can take when deciding what to do with an email:

1. Delete it – if it's a calendar notification, spam or someone cc'ing you as an FYI.
2. Reply to it – if it's going to take you less than a minute to respond, send that response immediately, then archive the email.

3. Write a longer reply – if you can't reply right now as a longer response is required, or you need more information before replying, write it as an action on your to-do list then file the email away until you get to that action item. It's a perilous game to use your inbox as a to-do list

4. Forward it to someone else to deal with – if you're not the best person to reply, send it on to the person who is and file the email.

As I said, this approach requires a daily dose of willpower; however, the benefits are so very worth it.

11. Everything takes longer than I expect it to

I hear you! I am a glass-half-full person myself, and this extends to my time management. I will *always* be optimistic about how long a task will take to complete – whether it's preparing dinner or getting to a meeting.

Some learnings I've had that may help you …

Time yourself

I recently read Sarah Knight's book *Get Your Sh*t Together* and she has a genius suggestion for those of us who tend to underestimate the time taken to do things. She advises us to time ourselves doing those everyday tasks that we *still* don't know exactly how long they take to do.

So we should set our timer on our phones to see how long it *really* takes us to have a shower and get dressed, or walk to the train station, or – and I love this – how long it takes us to leave the office. You know when you shut down your computer and you tell your partner that's when you're leaving? But you still need to pack up your bag, go to the bathroom, have a quick chat with a colleague ... In reality, you leave twelve minutes later.

I think this approach of timing ourselves is super-smart, because if we can get a handle on the actual amount of time we spend on those daily tasks, we're already getting closer to predicting our time more accurately.

Try the Pomodoro Technique

I talked about this clever time management technique in Chapter 12. The trick to engaging this approach successfully is to correctly estimate how many 'pomodoros' (i.e. blocks of twenty-five minutes) a task will take you. This comes with practice; however, it may give you a helpful system to more accurately forecast your time per task.

Allow buffer time

I generally plan my arrival at an appointment to the minute, which means that if I hit a snag (traffic, train delay, last minute phone call), I creep into 'five minutes late' territory.

My business partner Natalie is perennially punctual, and after observing her for a few weeks I realised why – she *always* allows herself buffer time to get somewhere. Rather than aiming to be at a 10 a.m. meeting at 10 a.m., she instead aims to be there at 9.40 a.m. This means that she is generally early, and arrives clear-minded and ready to go at whatever appointment she is attending.

I'm working on adopting her approach, and my – does it work! The added bonus is that when all goes to plan, I have twenty minutes of 'found time' to just think, send a few emails or do some additional prep for my meeting.

When we apply this approach to tasks, we allow more time than we think we'll need to get them completed.

If my Optimistic Time Angel thinks I could get that presentation for my speaking gig done in three hours, I should, in fact, allow five hours to keep my Pessimistic Time Angel happy. If I get the presentation done in four hours, I have a bonus hour up my sleeve.

Try overestimating the amount of time it will take to complete each task on your list by building in additional buffer time for yourself.

Be less perfect

I talked in Chapter 4 about the concept of 'satisficing', which means we get tasks to a point where they are completed, but not perfect. If you didn't know already, perfection doesn't exist.

There comes a certain point in every task where the amount of time we continue to put into it begins to have less of a return. Perhaps the first two hours that I spend working on a presentation gets it done to a basic level – the slides are there, there are some basic images and my key points are articulated. The third hour gets it up another notch – I've included some sexier images, now there are a couple of videos and some cool slide transitions. The fourth and fifth hour that I could then spend on it would probably see me fiddling with fonts, making the graphs more detailed and doing some animation whizzery.

Really, the presentation was looking pretty good after three hours; and the pay-off from those two extra hours is minimal. The font tweaks, fancier graphs and animations won't add much to my presentation and will be noticed by very few people. After three hours, it had reached the point of 'satisficient'.

Similarly with cleaning a house. In the first twenty minutes, we run around collecting up dirty dishes, making beds and picking clothes up off the floor. In the second twenty minutes, we vacuum the floors and clean the bathroom. In the third twenty minutes, we reconfigure the pantry and wipe out the fridge. For the purposes of feeling like our house isn't a pigsty, the first twenty minutes would do the trick. If we were to confidently welcome an unexpected visitor, the second twenty minutes would get us to that point. The third twenty minutes, we could probably live quite happily without – and could instead take twenty minutes to have a cup of tea and a slice of chocolate cake.

If tasks are taking you a whooooole lot longer than you expected them to take, ask yourself honestly whether you're being too much of a perfectionist with them. The most valuable time you can spend on a task is the first chunk of time; after that, the return for your investment of minutes or hours gradually declines.

Keep reading!

This is the part where I share the books that I have found helped me in the area of getting organised, which I have listed here for your reading pleasure should you wish to dive deeper into any of the concepts I've mentioned throughout this book.

Die Empty, Todd Henry
Read it for: A motivating read on how we can be our most brilliant every day, and avoid the stagnation that comes with knowing we're not operating at our full potential.

Do The Work, Steven Pressfield
Read it for: A motivating manifesto on overcoming procrastination, particularly when it comes to creative projects.
Note: I come back to the principles of this book constantly, especially when I'm decidedly outside my comfort zone on a project.

Eat That Frog!, Brian Tracy
Read it for: A guide to getting the difficult/shitty tasks done first every day, probably the biggest productivity hack of all time.

Flow, Mihaly Csikszentmihalyi
Read it for: An exploration of what it means to be in a 'flow state', and how to get there more often.

Get Your Sh*t Together, Sarah Knight
Read it for: A frank, absolutely hilarious guide to getting your life sorted. Sarah is like your wise but bad-ass BFF who only has your best interests in mind.

Making Habits, Breaking Habits, Jeremy Dean
Read it for: An investigation of how habits come about.

The 4-Hour Workweek, Tim Ferriss
Read it for: An insight into how Tim found multiple efficiencies in his business and life.
Note: Don't be fooled by the title, there are some organisational gems in here. You might also like to check out Tim's podcast and blog, where he shares his recent discoveries on success and efficiency.

The Life-Changing Magic of Tidying Up, Marie Kondo
Read it for: A decluttering bible. I completely understand why this book went on to garner cult status.

The Miracle Morning, Hal Elrod
Read it for: An insight into Hal's incredible story, and as a manual to building a morning routine that will have you jumping out of bed every day.

The Power of Habit, Charles Duhigg
Read it for: A scientific breakdown of how we form – and maintain – habits.

The Power of Less, Leo Babauta

Read it for: A brief and beautiful guide on having less 'stuff' in our lives, and finding small efficiencies day to day.

Note: Our past team members Rosalie and Emily went through a phase of having a cut-out of Leo's face stuck to their computer screens, and asking themselves constantly 'What would Leo do?' when they were struggling to be efficient.

The Sleep Revolution, Arianna Huffington

Read it for: A powerful campaign for why we need more sleep in our lives, and tips on how to get more.

The Now Habit, Neil Fiore

Read it for: A deeper understanding of why we procrastinate, especially how fear feeds procrastination.

The Seven Habits of Highly Effective People, Stephen R. Covey

Read it for: A blueprint to personal success. This is one of the original personal development books, and has stood the test of time since its first publication in 1988.

The Willpower Project, Kelly McGonigal

Read it for: An understanding of how willpower works, and how we can master it more in our lives.

Endnotes

Chapter 2: Declutter

1   Dolan, Erin, 'Scientists find physical clutter negatively affects your ability to focus, process information', unclutterer, 29 March 2011, <https://unclutterer.com/2011/03/29/scientists-find-physical-clutter-negatively-affects-your-ability-to-focus-process-information>.

2   Cho, Mikael, 'How Clutter Affects Your Brain (And What You Can Do About It)', lifehacker, 6 July 2013, <https://www.lifehacker.com.au/2013/07/how-clutter-affects-your-brain-and-what-you-can-do-about-it/#TPXRuXqecYPeyUw1.99>.

3   Chang, Charis 'Professional organiser Peter Walsh reveals why it's hard to let go of your stuff', news.com.au, 14 April 2016, <http://www.news.com.au/lifestyle/home/professional-organiser-peter-walsh-reveals-why-its-hard-to-let-go-of-your-stuff/news-story/ec6dcfd5e427a8625171ce4b024e8a28>.

4   Chang, Charis, 'The KonMari method for tidying up 'changes people's lives', news.com.au, 25 April 2015, <http://www.news.com.au/lifestyle/home/interiors/the-konmari-method-for-tidying-up-changes-peoples-lives/news-story/d95564f14d381db008569714b62e7956>.

Chapter 3: Basics

1   Covey, Stephen R., *The Seven Habits of Highly Effective People*, Business Library, Melbourne, 1990, p. 71.

2   Australian Transport Council 2011, *National Road Safety Strategy 2011–2020* <http://roadsafety.gov.au/nrss/>.

3   Transport Accident Commission, 'Fatigue Statistics', <http://www.tac.vic.gov.au/road-safety/statistics/summaries/fatigue-statistics>.

4   Giang, Vivian and Nisen, Max, 'See What The Desks Of 39 Successful People Look Like', Business Insider, 24 December 2013, <https://www.businessinsider.com.au/desks-of-famous-people-2013-1#now-see-what-future-workspaces-will-look-like-40>.

Chapter 4: Priorities and standards

1   Goins, Jeff, 'The Insanely Simple Way To Prioritize Your Work And Life', Fast Company, 20 May 2016, <https://www.fastcompany.com/3060031/the-insanely-simple-way-to-prioritize-your-work-and-life>.

2   Nastasi, Alison, 'How long does it *really* take to break a habit?' Hopes&Fears, <http://www.hopesandfears.com/hopes/now/question/216479-how-long-does-it-really-take-to-break-a-habit>.

3   'Guru: Herbert Simon', *The Economist*, 20 March 2009, <http://www.economist.com/node/13350892>.

4   Winfrey, Oprah, *What I Know for Sure*, Flatiron Books, New York, 2014, p. 71.

Chapter 5: The power of routine

1   Lally, Phillippa, et al, 'How are habits formed: Modelling habit formation in the real world', *European Journal of Social Psychology*, 40, 2010, pp 998–1009, < http://repositorio.ispa.pt/bitstream/10400.12/3364/1/IJSP_998-1009.pdf>.

Chapter 6: Morning routine

1   Wikipedia, 'White space (visual arts), https://en.wikipedia.org/wiki/White_space_(visual_arts)>.
2   Anxiety.org, 'Is your online addiction making you anxious?', 9 April 2016, <https://www.anxiety.org/social-media-causes-anxiety>.
3   Tatera, Kelly, 'New Study: The More You Use Social Media, The More Likely You Are to Be Depressed', The Science Explorer, 29 March 2016, <http://thescienceexplorer.com/brain-and-body/new-study-more-you-use-social-media-more-likely-you-are-be-depressed>.
4   DiSalvo, David, 'Your Brain Sees Even When You Don't', *Forbes*, 22 June 2013, <https://www.forbes.com/sites/daviddisalvo/2013/06/22/your-brain-sees-even-when-you-dont/#45af0d87116a>.
5   Morrissey, Mary, 'The Power of Writing Down Your Goals and Dreams' Huffington Post, 14 September 2016, <http://www.huffingtonpost.com/marymorrissey/the-power-of-writing-down_b_12002348.html>.
6   Elrod, Hal, *The Miracle Morning*, Hal Elrod International Inc., Temecula, 2012.

Chapter 8: Organising your week

1   Stack, Laura M., 'The Importance of Planning and Prioritizing', The Productivity Pro, 2000, <http://www.theproductivitypro.com/FeaturedArticles/article00017.htm>.
2   Taube, Aaron, 'Focusing On One Task At A Time Makes You 50% More Engaged At Work', Business Insider, 2 December 2014, <https://www.businessinsider.com.au/focusing-on-one-task-will-make-you-more-engaged-2014-12#CGcZpmCGw4dy5u6l.99>.
3   Smith, Jacquelyn, '16 things successful people do on Monday mornings', Business Insider, 2 June 2015, <https://www.businessinsider.com.au/what-successful-people-do-on-monday-mornings-2015-6#HT0FEfGteVY9Aii3.99>.

Chapter 10: Conquering distractions

1   Varney, Jorrie, 'Micro-generation born between 1977-1983 given new name', Sammiches & Psych Meds, 7 July 2017, <http://www.sammichespsychmeds.com/micro-generation-born-between-1977-1983-are-given-new-name>.
2   Cho, Mikael, 'How Clutter Affects Your Brain (And What You Can Do About It)', lifehacker, 6 July 2013, <https://www.lifehacker.com.au/2013/07/how-clutter-affects-your-brain-and-what-you-can-do-about-it/#TPXRuXqecYPeyUw1.99>.
3   Mark, Gloria, et al, 'The cost of interrupted work: More speed and stress', *Proceedings of the 2008 Conference on Human Factors in Computing Systems*, Florence, Italy, April 5–10, 2008, <https://www.researchgate.net/publication/221518077_The_cost_of_interrupted_work_More_speed_and_stress>.

Chapter 11: Outsourcing

1   Ham, Larissa, 'Outsourcing your life', Executive Style, <http://www.executivestyle.com.au/outsourcing-your-life-2ngg0#ixzz4poOp4ppY>.

Chapter 13: Family

1   Medoff, Lisa, 'Routines: Why They Matter and How to Get Started', Education.com, 6 August 2013, <https://www.education.com/magazine/article/importance-routines-preschool-children/>.

Words of appreciation

To the Hachette Australia team: *Remarkability* was life-changing for me. Thank you for backing me for a second adventure together. To Robert, my publisher, thank you for your trust and faith in me. Tom, my editor, you have once again made this book-making process a super-smooth and enjoyable experience; not easily done with a newborn! Thank you, Susin, for your wise and thorough copyediting of my manuscript. Sorry to make you change all your careful asterisks in 'f*ck' back to 'fuck' . . .

Thank you, Grace, for another stellar book cover – you have a way of capturing the very essence of my words and bringing them to life.

To my dear book researcher and assistant, Jo: you made this book a much more well-rounded entity and generally made me sound a bit clever, so thank you!

To Sally: I am so lucky to have your words adorning the front cover of this book. I cannot think of a person more suited to be in that spot – you blend a career in TV with authoring books, entrepreneuring at Swiish.com with Maha (seriously, what you guys achieve blows my mind) and being a gorgeous mama to Annabelle and Elyssa. You do it with such grace, no one would ever guess the graft that goes into every single day.

To Jacqui, Libby-Jane, Mike, Sally and Wade – thank you for providing your kind words for the opening pages of this book.

To the esteemed friends who answered my nosey questions for the purposes of this book: your willingness to share and your time is very much appreciated and I hope this behind-the-scenes look at how you run your terrifyingly successful lives will benefit many people who read it.

To my special team at The Remarkables Group: thank you for your bravery, support, faith, friendship and letting me nag you about double-sided printing and knuckle-cracking; not to mention the many delicious meals shared together.

To our dear clients at The Remarkables Group: this past year more than ever, thank you for your support as we completely changed our model. Special thanks to Mascha, Melanie, Sophie, Ruchi, Peter, Stephen, Toby, Carly, Penny, Jessica, Karlea, Kate, Lee and Ana. It's a special thing when you look forward to seeing your clients like you do your friends.

To my mentees – Jacqui, Cathy, Janine, Lisa, Kat, Brooke, Emily and Claire – thank you for entrusting me with your lives, businesses, wins and learnings. Speaking to you guys lights up my soul and I am deeply grateful for that opportunity.

To everyone who follows and interacts with me on social media: thank you for being on there and spending your precious time and energy following my life in this crazy, cool bubble we have online. I appreciate each and every one of you and your likes, comments, shares and messages. You guys are my tribe.

To the businesses (although 'movements' would probably be a more accurate term) who have supported me so much over the years: Collective Hub, Business Chicks and The Entourage, thank you – I feel like I'm a part of your teams.

To my parents: thank you for supporting Jenny and me in all that we do. Seeing you take on your new role as doting grandparents is very special to witness.

To my sister Jenny: thank you for being such a wonderful sister (and now auntie!). Talking about food, cooking food and eating food – while talking about more food – with you is a delight. I just wish we got to do it more often.

To Barry and Janet, and all of Wade's family: thank you for making me a part of your family.

To Team Lexi: from our doula, Nadine, and midwife, Jo, to our nanny, Iva, and the many friends and family who have supported Wade, Lexi and me on this new adventure as parents – thank you from the bottom of our hearts. That this has been such a joy-filled and much-easier-than-expected transition is a testament to your love, wisdom and care for the three of us.

To the divine force: you continue to surprise and thrill me with the breaks, and the opportunities to grow (AKA the tough times!), that you send my way. Thank you for the big miracles and the small ones too.

To Jacqui (or, as I see you, my secret weapon): thank you for your monthly TLC, and for being there in between when I need some extra tuning up. You keep me on course, connected and calm-ish.

To my partner in life, Wade: we certainly have not chosen the easy road, you and me! Two entrepreneurs and a tiny baby certainly makes for an interesting life, and I wouldn't have it any other way. I cannot adequately express how it feels to know you have my back in everything I do.

To my daughter, Lexi: I still cannot believe we get to keep you! You are pure magic, little one. Thank you for being the chilled rockstar you are, and for being so kind to Daddy and me. I don't think you'll ever fully know how loved you are by us, and so many others.

To you, the reader: thank you for investing your precious time to read this book with me. I so hope you have reached the last pages with some clear actions – not to mention the motivation – to get remarkably organised. I promise you your life will be all the richer and happier for it. I cannot tell you how much I love to hear your feedback, so please stay in touch.

lorrainemurphy.com.au
⊙ @lorraineremarks
◼ /lorraineremarks
Facebook group: 'Get Remarkably Organised'

Lorraine Murphy is an award-winning entrepreneur and author. In 2012, she founded The Remarkables Group, a pioneering influencer strategy agency. Prior to starting The Remarkables Group, Lorraine created and managed campaigns in an eight-year PR career that began in Dublin, moved to London and ended up in Sydney where she now lives and works. Lorraine's acclaimed bestselling first book, *Remarkability*, was published in 2016.